MY COUNTRY MY GOVERNMENT

This book is a collection of four books—*The Constitution* (2001), *The Executive Council* (2002), *The Legislature* (2003) and *The Judiciary* (2003)—first published by Scholastic India.

Published by Scholastic India Pvt. Ltd.
A subsidiary of Scholastic Inc., New York, 10012 (USA).
Publishers since 1920, with international operations in Canada,
Australia, New Zealand, the United Kingdom, India, and Hong Kong.

For information regarding permission, write to:
Scholastic India Pvt. Ltd.
A-27, Ground Floor, Bharti Sigma Centre
Infocity-1, Sector 34, Gurgaon-122001 (India)

First edition: April 2019
This reprint edition: July 2025

ISBN-13: 978-93-5275-733-6

Printed in India at Shivam Offset Press, New Delhi

MY COUNTRY MY GOVERNMENT

ROHINI OOMMAN

Illustrations by
Atanu Roy and Fazbi Shamnath

SCHOLASTIC
New York Toronto London Auckland
Sydney New Delhi Hong Kong

THE CONSTITUTION 1-29

THE UNION EXECUTIVE 31-66

THE LEGISLATURE

67-96

THE JUDICIARY

97-136

THE CONSTITUTION

WHAT IS A CONSTITUTION?

In any country there has to be a set of rules that is above all other laws otherwise citizens will not be able to claim their rights nor will the government be able to enforce its laws. This law is called the **Constitution.** Our Constitution is the **highest law of the land** and cannot be changed at the whim of a government or an individual. It has to be done through a legal process through an **amendment** in Parliament.

WHY HAVE A CONSTITUTION?

A basic law of the land is needed to spell out various questions raised when forming a government.

In any country the following questions will arise:

- Who is a citizen?
- What are the rights of a citizen?
- What are the duties of a citizen?
- How should government be organised: as a federal or a unitary structure?
- What type of a government should be established: parliamentary or presidential?
- What are the powers and functions of the different branches of government: the legislature, the executive and the judiciary?
- How should the head of the government be elected?
- Can the head of the government be in office forever? Can he be dismissed? If so, how and by whom?
- What should be the procedure to change the Constitution?

These and many other issues will be explained and documented in a Constitution. One of the rules spelt out will be the conditions for amending a Constitution. A Constitution reflects the aspirations of the people who draw up the document. It outlines the powers and functions of a government and the rights and duties of the citizens.

CAN YOU TELL?

How is a Constitution different from other laws?

WHO IS AN INDIAN CITIZEN?

According to the Indian Constitution, an Indian citizen is a person

i) who is born on Indian territory;
ii) either of whose parents was born on Indian territory;
iii) who has been a resident of India for five years immediately preceding the commencement of the Constitution.

CAN YOU TELL?

Which of these are citizens of India?

i) My ancestors from India left India 200 years ago and I live in the West Indies.
ii) Although, I now live in Mumbai, I was born in the United States and my parents Kamala and Ram Suri are Indian citizens.
iii) Mr D'Sousa lives in Goa. His ancestors came from Portugal to India 600 years ago.
iv) Mr Shroff's Zoroastrian ancestors settled in Gujarat 1000 years ago.
v) Mr Irani, a Zoroastrian came to India from Iran five years ago.
vi) Mr John Smith, an Englishman, has been living in India since 1944.

WHAT DOES THE CONSTITUTION OF INDIA SAY?

WHO FRAMED THE CONSTITUTION?
The Constitution was drawn up by a group of people who were elected as members of the **Constituent Assembly**. They represented the different people of India: Muslims, Sikhs, Anglo-Indians, Indian Christians, Parsees, Scheduled Castes and Tribes. The Chairman of the Drafting Committee of the Constitution was Dr. B.R. Ambedkar. Although the Constitution was enacted in 1949 it came into force on 26th January 1950.

PREAMBLE TO THE CONSTITUTION

WE, THE PEOPLE OF INDIA,
having solemnly resolved to constitute India into a **SOVEREIGN, SOCIALIST, SECULAR, DEMOCRATIC REPUBLIC** and to secure to all its citizens:
JUSTICE, social, economic and political;
LIBERTY of thought, expression, belief, faith, and worship;
EQUALITY of status and of opportunity;
and to promote among them all
FRATERNITY assuring the dignity of the individual and the unity and integrity of the Nation;
IN OUR CONSTITUENT ASSEMBLY this twenty-sixth day of November, 1949, do **HEREBY ADOPT, ENACT AND GIVE TO OURSELVES THIS CONSTITUTION.**

CAN YOU TELL?
What do we celebrate on the 26th of January? What is the significance of that day?

HOW IS OUR GOVERNMENT ORGANISED?

The **PREAMBLE** is an introduction to the Constitution. The Preamble sets down the **PLAN** of how our government is to be organised. It also sets down the **AIMS AND OBJECTIVES** that governments must strive to achieve for its citizens.

PLAN OF OUR GOVERNMENT: The framers of our Constitution wanted India to be a: *Sovereign, Socialist, Secular, Democratic Republic.* Read the definitions on pages 29-30.

CAN YOU TELL?

1. Which terms are opposite in meaning of the following concepts?
   Dictatorship, Monarchy, Capitalistic, Theocratic, Colonial state

Sovereign State	
Socialist	
Secular	
Democracy	
Republic	

2 The date on which India became a sovereign, democratic republic

----

3 Find out which amendment added the words **Socialist, Secular** and **integrity of the Nation** to the Preamble. Why do you think these words were added later?

----

4 Quote the words from the Preamble that show the source from where the Constitution gets its power

----

5 Name one country that is a theocratic state

----

6 What does fraternity mean?

RECOGNISING DEFINITIONS

Look up the meaning of the following terms:
sovereignty, socialism, secularism, democratic republic, dictatorship, monarchy, capitalism, theocracy, and colonial state
Select the term that best defines the idea in Column 1 and enter it in Column 2

COLUMN 1	COLUMN 2
India does not sign a treaty banning the testing of nuclear weapons.	
When the Indian Railways incurs a loss it tries to keep the cost of a second class railway ticket affordable for the common man.	
In 1942, Britain decided that Indian soldiers had to fight Britain's war against Germany, Italy and Japan.	
The laws of a country reflect the beliefs of all communities and are not based on any one religion.	
Elections in India are held on the basis of Universal Adult Franchise.	
The Head of the State is the President of India elected through an Electorl College.	
Mohammed bin Salman Al Saud of Saudi Arabia is also the Prime Minister and the Commander of the National Guard.	
All laws in the Islamic Republic of Iran are strongly influenced by Shiite Muslim clerics.	
In the United States, Private enterprises provide utilities like electricity, water and telephone.	
The Government of a country is managed by military chief.	

WHAT IS THE STRUCTURE OF GOVERNMENT IN INDIA?

INDIA IS : A **Democratic Republic** and a **Federal State**.

A DEMOCRATIC FEDERAL REPUBLIC implies :

i) that the government of a state is made up of elected representatives and the citizens of the state enjoy basic freedoms,

ii) that the country is divided into several units: **states** with their own governments,

iii) that the head of the state is elected.

CAN YOU TELL?

Which of the features in the box

(a) are essential features of a democratic state?

(b) indicate that India is a Republic?

(c) indicate that India is a Federal State?

Mark column 2 below with the appropriate symbols:

D=democratic **R=republic** **F=federal**

		D	R	F
i)	an elected head of state–the President			
ii)	elected representatives to make laws–the legislature			
iii)	a judiciary that is separate from the executive and the legislature			
iv)	a system of fair and free elections			
v)	Universal Adult Franchise–the right to vote			
vi)	a Constitution that guarantees equality and freedom			
vii)	a division of the state into smaller units with the sharing of political power between a Central Government and several independent State Governments.			

WHAT ARE THE AIMS OF OUR CONSTITUTION?

INDIA → Democratic State

One of the **AIMS** of the Indian Constitution is to provide for all its citizens: Justice, Liberty, Equality, Fraternity

In a **Democratic State** it is the **people** who vote for their representatives to the government. As the government is formed by a party or a group of parties with the largest number of elected members, it is the rule of the majority. Therefore, there is a risk that laws framed might take into account only the interests of the majority group. The **RIGHTS** of the minority must be protected through equal participation of all citizens in the voting process–**Universal Adult Franchise**. Everyone over 18 has the right to vote. In a democracy the **law is the same for everyone**. It should be applied in the same way to all. People who are not in power must be allowed to speak out against injustice–**freedom of expression.** Everyone has the right to live in **freedom.** As India is a multi-cultural, multi-religious society with a diversity of people with differing viewpoints, everyone's **rights** must be protected. Our Constitution provides for six rights, that are:

I) **fundamental** to human nature

II) **fundamental** to a democratic political system

The **SEVEN** rights are

i) Right to Equality
ii) Right to Freedom
iii) Right against Exploitation
iv) Right to Freedom of Religion
v) Cultural and Educational Rights
vi) Right to Constitutional Remedies
vii) Right to Education

The seventh right is to provide free and compulsory education to all children in the age group of six to fourteen years

CAN YOU TELL?

Which right allows Mr. Rao to file a suit against the Government for closing down his printing press?

FUNDAMENTAL RIGHTS

ARTICLE 14: The State shall not deny to any person equality before the law or the equal protection of the laws within the territory of India.
ARTICLE 15: Prohibition of discrimination on grounds of religion, race, caste, sex or place of birth.

The State shall not discriminate against any citizen on grounds only of religion, race, caste, sex, place of birth or any of them and deny:

(i) access to shops, public restaurants, hotels and places of public entertainment; or

(ii) the use of wells, tanks, bathing ghats, roads and places of public resort maintained wholly or partly out of State funds or dedicated to the use of the general public.

The State can make special provisions for women and children.
The State can make special provision for the advancement of any socially and educationally backward classes of citizens or for the Scheduled Castes and the Scheduled Tribes.

CAN YOU TELL?

Which kind of discrimination is/was practised in the examples given below?

1 In 1960, Rosa Parks, a black woman was not allowed to sit in the front of a bus in Alabama.
2 The Turks massacred the Armenians in 1915-1916 and took away part of their land and added it to Turkey.
3 Earlier, Air India did not employ women as air–hostesses after they were married.
4 In many villages in India there are two sets of wells located in different parts of the village. The upper caste people do not allow others to use their well.
5 In many Western countries a work permit is often denied to people not of European or Western origin.
6 In 1994, in Rwanda, the Tutsi tribe was massacred by the Hutu tribe, forcing the Tutsis to flee to neighbouring countries.
7 In the 1940's, a person of Jewish faith had to be registered with the German Government.
8 In 1990, in Bosnia Herzogovina, part of what was Yugoslavia, the Serbs massacred the Croats and the Muslims.

Think of some examples of similar discrimination based on colour, race, caste, religion, sex, place of birth.

FIND OUT

Is reservation of seats for backward classes in professional colleges like engineering and medical a violation of Article 15?

ARTICLE 19: Protection of certain rights regarding freedom of speech, etc.

1. All citizens shall have the right–
   (a) to freedom of speech and expression;
   (b) to assemble peaceably and without arms;
   (c) to form associations or unions;
   (d) to move freely throughout the territory of India;
   (e) to reside and settle in any part of the territory of India; and
   (g) to practise any profession, or to carry on any occupation, trade or business.

ARTICLE 21: Protection of life and personal liberty.

No person shall be deprived of his life or personal liberty except according to procedure established by law.

CAN YOU TELL?

Which Fundamental Right has been infringed upon in the following situations?

A movie has been banned because the Director has criticised Government's inaction during a riot.	
A government issues a directive that all members of a minority group have to carry special identity cards.	
They have killed my two sons, my wife and my only daughter along with three others all because we have been refusing to do menial jobs in our village that we had been carrying on for decades...	
In an increasing number of schools in Ahmedabad and elsewhere, there is no choice for the Muslims—exams are held even on Eid, so both the students and the teachers have to be present.	

WHICH FUNDAMENTAL RIGHTS PROTECT THE MINORITIES?

ARTICLE 25: Freedom of conscience and free profession, practice and propagation of religion.
ARTICLE 26: Freedom to manage religious affairs.
ARTICLE 27: Freedom as to payment of taxes for promotion of any particular religion.
ARTICLE 28: Freedom as to attendance at religious instruction or religious worship in certain educational institutions.

CAN YOU TELL?

Study the table of population distribution by religion.

1 Which religion is followed by the majority of people in India?
2 Arrange the religions in descending order of percentage distribution.

Population by religion 2011

Hindu	79.80 %	96.62 Crores	28
Muslim	14.23 %	17.22 Crores	2
Christian	2.30 %	2.78 Crores	4
Sikh	1.72 %	2.08 Crores	1
Buddhist	0.70 %	84.43 Lakhs	-
Jain	0.37 %	44.52 Lakhs	-
Other Religion	0.66 %	79.38 Lakhs	-
Not Stated	0.24 %		

*Excluding J&K, †Excluding Assam.

DID YOU KNOW?

In the Constitution the reference to Hindus is interpreted as all persons professing the Hindu, Sikh, Jain and Buddhist religions.

FIND OUT

When did Christianity, Islam, Zoroastrianism and Judaism first establish itself in India?

ARTICLE 29: Protection of interests of minorities.

1 Any section of the citizens residing in the territory of India or any part thereof having a distinct language, script or culture of its own shall have the right to conserve the same.
2 No citizen shall be denied admission into any educational institution maintained by the State or receiving aid out of State funds on grounds only of religion, race, caste, language or any of them.

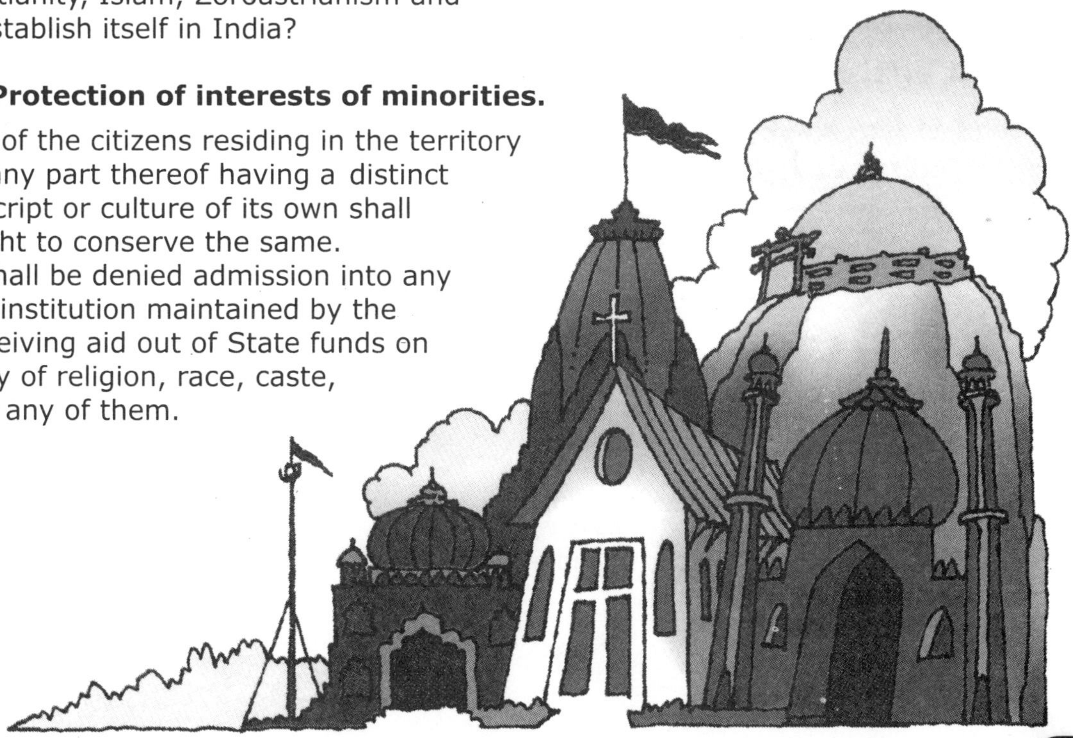

ARTICLE 30: Right of minorities to establish and administer educational institutions.
All minorities, whether based on religion or language, shall have the right to establish and administer educational institutions of their choice.

TEST YOUR COMPREHENSION SKILLS

1 Refer to page 8 and name three Fundamental Rights that protect the **freedom of minorities** in India?

i)..

ii)..

iii)..

2 Can the Government pass a law ordering all private schools and colleges to admit students only from the neighbourhood? Give reasons.

....

....

Right against Exploitation

Think of two ways in which

1. children are exploited in India.

....

....

2. women are exploited in India.

....

....

3. poor people are exploited in India.

....

....

ARE FUNDAMENTAL RIGHTS ABSOLUTE?

No right is fixed or absolute. Each country has framed its own set of fundamental rights according to the social and economic conditions that exist in the country.
These change from time to time and so, as the need arises, more rights can be added to fundamental rights through an amendment. The right to education is being considered as a fundamental right.

Fundamental Rights can be suspended:

1 If a general Emergency is imposed in times of war or during other crisis situations like riots in the country, the President can suspend some or all Fundamental Rights—even the right to Constitutional remedies.

2 If there is a threat to public health. If we were struck by an infectious disease as threatening as ebola or plague, then a Fundamental Right like freedom to move throughout the territory of India may be suspended.

3 If a citizen through immoral actions harms other citizens then his/her rights could be suspended as in the case of drug trafficking.

There are restrictions on the Right to Freedom if there is a threat to:

i) the sovereignty and integrity of India,

ii) the security of the State,

iii) friendly relations with foreign states,

iv) public order, decency or morality,

v) or in relation to contempt of court, defamation or incitement to an offence.

CAN YOU TELL?

Can Cabaret dancers working in bars challenge the Government's authority to raid bars and arrest them for stripping?

The Indian Constitution is the only Constitution in the world that has stated Fundamental Duties.

Good citizenship also means respecting other people's rights. An individual's Fundamental Right should not violate the rights of other citizens. In the guise of freedom of expression a citizen cannot slander another individual and spoil his reputation. Make a list of your own, on what you think your duties as a good citizen should be. Fundamental Rights cannot be taken away by an ordinary law. They can be amended only by a special majority in Parliament.

WHICH RIGHTS ARE FUNDAMENTAL TO HUMAN NATURE?

The Universal Declaration of Human Rights (1948) declares that every human being has the right to live in dignity. The rights are described in 30 articles of the Universal Declaration of Human Rights. Regardless of sex, colour of the skin, language, religion, caste, economic class, different beliefs, or coming from another country, whether the country you live in is independent or not, these rights are essential to uphold the dignity of a person:

i) Right to life, liberty and safety of person;
ii) Right to freedom of conscience and religion;
iii) Right to freedom of opinion, expression, association, and assembly;
iv) Right to freedom from arbitrary arrest; to a fair and impartial trial;
v) Right to freedom from interference in privacy, home, or correspondence;
vi) Right to a nationality;
vii) Right to a secure society and an adequate standard of living;
viii) Right to education;
ix) Right to rest and leisure.

ARTICLE 38: The State to secure a social order for the promotion of welfare of the people.
This article states that the Government will strive to promote the welfare of the people by securing and protecting as effectively as it may a society in which there is justice, social, economic and political.

Given the problems mentioned above, selecting rights as fundamental for the Indian Constitution was a difficult choice for members of the Constituent Assembly. There were various social and economic problems that could not be ignored but the Government of India did not have the means to promise certain human rights. Many of these rights were incorporated into a list of goals for the government to achieve through legislation. These long run objectives of the Government of India were referred to as: **The Directive Principles of State Policy.**

WHY DO WE NEED DIRECTIVE PRINCIPLES IN OUR CONSTITUTION?

India has a parliamentary form of government. Every five years people elect a new government. The government is formed of elected members from the party that wins the most votes. The other parties form the opposition to the government. Sometimes, because of a vote of no confidence in the government, the government is toppled before its term is completed. Changing governments means change in policies. Certain goals and objectives ensuring the well being of all the people have to be kept in mind when framing policies. To quote the Constitution—

'The principles laid down are nevertheless fundamental in the governance of the country and it shall be the duty of the State to apply these principles in making laws.'

What distinguishes Fundamental Rights from Directive Principles?

A citizen can claim Fundamental Rights through a court of law.

Directive Principles cannot be enforced in a court of law. To make a directive principle enforceable it must first be made a law by passing a bill in parliament.

CAN YOU TELL?

1. Can a citizen challenge the Government in a court of law and claim compensation for unemployment?
2. Can a citizen who has been denied the right to publish a newspaper claim the right through a court of law?
3. Can workers claim minimum wages and compensation for sickness, accidents etc. as a Fundamental Right?

CAN YOU IDENTIFY EXAMPLES OF SOCIAL, ECONOMIC AND POLITICAL INJUSTICE?

Refer to Pages 26-28 and make a list of the Directive Principles you think should be a Fundamental Right. Keep in mind the practical aspects of implementing such a right.

The table below provides some examples of injustice. Mark the given examples as:
S = social; E = economic; P = political.

EXAMPLE		INJUSTICE
i)	Children working in carpet factories	
ii)	Unequal wages for men and women doing the same work	
iii)	Harassment for dowry	
iv)	Indiscriminate killing of Dalits by upper caste groups	
v)	Good private schools and badly equipped government schools	
vi)	Inability to seek legal aid because of low incomes	
vii)	Denial of justice because of delays in settling disputes through courts	
viii)	People not being able to exercise voting rights because of illiteracy and poverty	
ix)	A rich man's son is not convicted of manslaughter because he pays off witnesses	
x)	The common man held as a prisoner indefinitely on suspicion of being involved in disruptive activities	
xi)	A civil code that works unfavourably for women	
xii)	Children working as domestic help	

HOW MANY STATES DO WE HAVE IN THE FEDERATION OF INDIA?

India is a federation of 28 states. Can you name all of them? How many different states have you lived in? How many different languages can you speak?

1. Andhra Pradesh	11.	21.
2.	12.	22.
3.	13.	23.
4.	14.	24.
5.	15.	25.
6.	16.	26.
7.	17.	27.
8.	18.	28.
9.	19.	
10.	20.	

UNION TERRITORIES

Besides the 28 States there are 8 Union Territories. The Central Government administers the Union Territories directly through an administrator or a Lieutenant Governor.

1. Andaman & Nicobar Islands	2. Chandigarh	7. National Capital Territory
3. Dadra and Nagar Haveli and Daman & Diu	4. Puducherry	8. Ladakh
5. Lakshadweep	6. Jammu and Kashmir	

Earlier Delhi was a Union Territory but in 1991, it was declared a National Capital Territory with its own Legislative Assembly.

CAN YOU TELL WHY?

Earlier, The Constitution read as follows:
We the **PEOPLE OF INDIA,** having solemnly resolved to constitute India into a **SOVEREIGN, DEMOCRATIC REPUBLIC** . . .
FRATERNITY assuring the dignity of the individual and the unity of the nation . . .
The words: **socialist** and **secular** had been omitted earlier from the Constitution. The word **integrity** was later added to the Constitution to read as: unity and integrity of the nation.

HOW IS GOVERNMENT POWER SHARED?

India, as a Federal State comprises 29 States each with its own government. The three newly formulated States are still in the process of becoming autonomous. The Constitution has distributed the powers of the government between the State Government and the Central or Union Government in the following manner:

The Union Government
The Union List

The State Government
The State List

The Concurrent List
We both make laws on subjects common to both

Any other matter that is not listed either in the State list or the Concurrent list is also a matter for the Union government.

UNION LIST	STATE LIST	CONCURRENT LIST
Defence of India	Law and order within the State	Marriage and divorce, adoption, wills
Central Bureau of Intelligence	Police	Bankruptcy and insolvency
Foreign Affairs	Local Government powers and institutions	Lunacy and mental deficiency
War and peace	Public health and sanitation	Prevention of cruelty to animals
Railways	Roads, bridges and ferries within the state	Forests
Post and Telegraph	Regulation of mines	Protection of Wildlife
Citizenship	Betting and gambling	Adulteration of food stuff
Entering into treaties and agreements	Taxes on agricultural income	Population control and Family planning
Reserve Bank of India	Taxes on land and buildings	Legal, medical and other professions
Ancient and historical monuments	Taxes on vehicles	Drugs and poisons
National highways	Elections to State legislatures	Electricity

HOW POWERFUL ARE THE STATES OF THE UNION OF INDIA?

1 The Union Government has the power to make laws on 52 subjects listed in the Concurrent list and some that are of regional concern.

2 If a State Law on any of these subjects is in conflict with the Union Law, the Union Law prevails.

3 The Union Government can overrule the authority of the States both in abnormal and peace times. The President can declare an emergency and during an emergency the powers of the State Government are curtailed.

CAN YOU TELL?

How do you think power should be shared?

1 Is political power more centralised or decentralised in the Indian Federation?

2 The army comes under the authority of the Union Government.

i) Why is 'Police' listed as a State subject?

ii) What are the disadvantages of police being a State subject?

Which Government, Union or State will make laws for:

	Subject	Government
1	Making the study of the regional language compulsory	
2	An increase in sales tax	
3	Granting benefits to the police force	
4	An increase in defence personnel's salaries	
5	Collecting tolls for the use of flyovers in a city	
6	Laws banning the shooting of wildlife	
7	Levying fines for defacing historical monuments	
8	Increasing the postage rate	
9	Increasing railway fares	

FRATERNITY AS ONE OF THE GOALS OF THE CONSTITUTION

India is a **multi-cultural** society. A community can be defined as a group which shares some cultural features. In India we have communities based on language, religion, customs, tradition, caste, class and other social groups. India has 22 officially recognised languages and more than 19,000 languages or dialects are spoken. Name the States where the following languages are spoken by a large majority or a large number of people:

1. Assamese	
2. Bengali	
3. Gujarati	
4. Hindi	
5. Kannada	
6. Kashmiri	
7. Konkani	
8. Malayalam	
9. Manipuri	
10. Marathi	
11. Nepali /Gorkhali	
12. Oriya	
13. Punjabi	
14. Sindhi	
15. Tamil	
16. Telugu	
17. Urdu	

HOW MULTI-CULTURAL IS INDIAN SOCIETY?

Even though each State has a regional language it officially recognises, there are many other linguistic groups living within the State. Find out which community speaks the following languages and in which States:

Tulu ____________ **Kodagu** ____________ **Dogri** ____________

Besides linguistic groups, name different religious and social communities in the state you live in.

THE REPUBLIC OF INDIA

A republic is a country where the Head of State is elected as a representative of the people as opposed to a hereditary office as in England or a dictatorship of an individual or a party.

In a republic

- The power of government is held by people.
- People give power to leaders they elect to represent them and serve their interests.

Some political systems have a hereditary head of state, for instance, Great Britain. Britain is not a republic but a **monarchy** because the head of the state, the king or queen is a **hereditary** office. However, a country that has a constitution that limits the power of the monarchy is referred to as a **Constitutional Monarchy**. Britain is a Constitutional Monarchy and a democratic state. People elect the Members of Parliament. The powers of the King or Queen are limited by the Constitution.

India is a **Republic:**

i) The Head of Government, the **Prime Minister** is directly elected.
ii) The Office of the Chief of State—the **President** is not an inherited office but an elected office.

A Republic is not always a Democratic State.
A Republic may or may not be a democracy, depending on voting qualifications, the degree of suffrage—who has the right to vote, as in some Communist countries such as China.
A democracy is a republic when PEOPLE ELECT the Head of State and the Head of Government.

IS THE STATE A:

FIND OUT:

IDENTIFY THE TYPE OF STATE IN THE COUNTRIES LISTED BELOW:

Afghanistan		Ireland		Pakistan	
Australia		Israel		Saudi Arabia	
Bangladesh		Japan		Sri Lanka	
Bhutan		Kenya		Sweden	
China		Kuwait		United Kingdom	
France		Myanmar		United States of America	
Iran		Nepal		Zaire	
Iraq		Nigeria			

Democracy – DM
Democratic Republic – DR
Constitutional Monarchy – CM
Dictatorship – DC
Republic in name – RN
Monarchy – M

WHICH OF THESE RIGHTS ARE ESSENTIAL TO A DEMOCRACY?

These are the words of President Roosevelt, US Democratic politician, from a speech delivered to the Congress on 6 January 1941, during World War II. It was his hope that the freedoms referred to would be achieved in the years to follow:

'We look forward to a world founded upon four essential human freedoms. The first is freedom of speech and expression everywhere in the world. The second is freedom of every person to worship God in his own way everywhere in the world. The third is freedom from want . . . everywhere in the world. The fourth is freedom from fear . . . anywhere in the world.'

Discuss how far these expectations have been fulfilled in the last 50 years? Discuss not only with reference to India but to other countries as well.

DEMOCRACY IN DANGER

When citizens are **denied liberty** of thought, expression, belief, faith and worship; and there is discrimination on grounds of class, caste, colour, creed, community and sex, then **democracy is at risk.**

In China, in 1989, students gathered in Tienanmien Square in Beijing to protest against the Chinese Government's policies. They demanded political reform and liberalisation in their country. The Chinese Government opened fire on them and many students were killed, many fled the country and many are still in jail.

In Myanmar, the leader of the political party—the *National League for Democracy*, Aung San Suu Kyi has been kept under house arrest because of her criticism of the military dictatorship.

In Odisha in 1999, an Australian Christian missionary, Graham Staines working among tribal people was burnt to death because of his missionary work. The jeep in which he and his two sons were sleeping was set on fire.

A journalist's office was ransacked and destroyed because he published an incriminating report on a politican in India.

The Nuremberg Race Laws in Germany, in 1933, discriminated against the Jews taking away their rights. The laws stipulated that all Jewish people wear a yellow star for identification; forbade Jews to own dogs, use public parks or swimming pools. Such laws herded Jews to live in ghettos; prevented Jews from holding public office, or undertaking any professional work as teachers, lawyers, doctors, publishers, editors.

CAN YOU TELL?

What kind of government is it that tells you what to do, what to say, what to see, how to behave, what to think and what to believe justifying such measures in the name of patriotism?

Select the appropriate answers from the following words and mark a tick in the box.

☐ Conservative	☐ Fascist	☐ Egalitarian	☐ Authoritarian
☐ Nationalistic	☐ Liberal	☐ Progressive	☐ Dictatorship

FIND OUT OTHER HAPPENINGS IN THE WORLD WHERE DEMOCRACY IS AT RISK?

ARTICLE 1 A: FUNDAMENTAL DUTIES

It shall be the duty of every citizen of India–

(a) to abide by the Constitution and respect its ideals and institutions, the National Flag and the National Anthem;
(b) to cherish and follow the noble ideals which inspired our national struggle for freedom;
(c) to uphold and protect the sovereignty, unity and integrity of India;
(d) to defend the country and render national service when called upon to do so;
(e) to promote harmony and the spirit of common brotherhood amongst all the people of India transcending religious, linguistic and regional or sectional diversities; to renounce practices derogatory to the dignity of women;
(f) to value and preserve the rich heritage of our composite culture;
(g) to protect and improve the natural environment including forests, lakes, rivers and wildlife, and to have compassion for living creatures;
(h) to develop the scientific temper, humanism and the spirit of inquiry and reform;
(i) to safeguard public property and to abjure violence;
(j) to strive towards excellence in all spheres of individual and collective activity so that the nation constantly rises to higher levels of endeavour and achievement.

DIRECTIVE PRINCIPLES OF STATE POLICY

Directive Principles of State policy as stated in **Articles 37 to Article 51** are **GUIDELINES** for goals to be achieved by all governments, present and future. These guidelines endeavour to assure citizens of India of their right to live with dignity and enjoy economic, social and political freedom.

ARTICLE 37: Application of the principles contained in this Part.
The provisions contained in this Part shall not be enforceable by any court, but the principles therein laid down are nevertheless fundamental in the governance of the country and it shall be the duty of the State to apply these principles in making laws. [(2) The State shall, in particular, strive to minimise the inequalities in income, and endeavour to eliminate inequalities in status, facilities and opportunities, not only amongst individuals but also amongst groups of people residing in different areas or engaged in different vocations.]

ARTICLE 39: Certain principles of policy to be followed by the State.
The State shall, in particular, direct its policy towards securing–

(a) that the citizens, men and women equally, have the right to an adequate means of livelihood;
(b) that the ownership and control of the material resources of the community are so distributed as best to serve the common good;

(c) that the operation of the economic system does not result in the concentration of wealth and means of production to the common detriment;

(d) that there is equal pay for equal work for both men and women;

(e) that the health and strength of workers, men and women, and the tender age of children are not abused and that citizens are not forced by economic necessity to enter vocations unsuited to their age or strength;

(f) that children are given opportunities and facilities to develop in a healthy manner and in conditions of freedom and dignity and that childhood and youth are protected against exploitation and against moral and material abandonment.

ARTICLE 39A: Equal justice and free legal aid.

ARTICLE 40: Organisation of village panchayats.

The State shall take steps to organise village panchayats and endow them with such powers and authority as may be necessary to enable them to function as units of self-government.

ARTICLE 41: Right to work, to education and to public assistance in certain cases.

The State shall, within the limits of its economic capacity and development, make effective provision for securing the right to work, to education and to public assistance in cases of unemployment, old age, sickness and disablement, and in other cases of undeserved want.

ARTICLE 42: Provision for just and humane conditions of work and maternity relief.

The State shall make provision for securing just and humane conditions of work and for maternity relief.

ARTICLE 43: Living wage, etc., for workers.

The State shall endeavour to secure, by suitable legislation or economic organisation or in any other way, to all workers, agricultural, industrial or otherwise, work, a living wage, conditions of work ensuring a decent standard of life and full enjoyment of leisure and social and cultural opportunities and, in particular, the State shall endeavour to promote cottage industries on an individual or co-operative basis in rural areas.

ARTICLE 43A: Participation of workers in management of industries.

The State shall take steps, by suitable legislation or in any other way, to secure the participation of workers in the management of undertakings, establishments or other organisations engaged in any industry.

ARTICLE 44: Uniform civil code for the citizens.

The State shall endeavour to secure for the citizens a uniform civil code throughout the territory of India.

ARTICLE 45: Provision for free and compulsory education for children.

The State shall endeavour to provide, within a period of ten years from the commencement of this Constitution, for free and compulsory education for all children until they complete the age of fourteen years.

ARTICLE 46: Promotion of educational and economic interests of Scheduled Castes, Scheduled Tribes and other weaker sections.

The State shall promote with special care the educational and economic interests of the weaker sections of the people, and, in particular, of the Scheduled Castes and the Scheduled Tribes, and shall protect them from social injustice and all forms of exploitation.

ARTICLE 47: Duty of the State to raise the level of nutrition and the standard of living and to improve public health.

ARTICLE 48: Organisation of agriculture and animal husbandry.

The State shall endeavour to organise agriculture and animal husbandry on modern and scientific lines and shall, in particular, take steps for preserving and improving the breeds, and prohibiting the slaughter, of cows and calves and other milch and draught cattle.

ARTICLE 48A: Protection and improvement of environment and safeguarding of forests and wildlife.

The State shall endeavour to protect and improve the environment and to safeguard the forests and wildlife of the country.

ARTICLE 49: Protection of monuments and places and objects of national importance.

It shall be the obligation of the State to protect every monument or place or object of artistic or historic interest, [declared by or under law made by Parliament] to be of national importance, from spoilation, disfigurement, destruction, removal, disposal or export, as the case may be.

ARTICLE 50: Separation of judiciary from executive.

The State shall take steps to separate the judiciary from the executive in the public services of the State.

ARTICLE 51: Promotion of international peace and security.

The State shall endeavour to–

(a) promote international peace and security;
(b) maintain just and honourable relations between nations;
(c) foster respect for international law and treaty obligations in the dealings of organised peoples with one another; and
(d) encourage settlement of international disputes by arbitration.

IMPORTANT WORDS AND TERMS

Amendment is any change in the Constitution.

Articles state the precise intentions of the Constitution.

Capitalist State: A state where production of goods and services is determined by market forces that is by the demand and supply for a product. The price of goods and services is determined by market forces and not by the Government. Therefore, the factors that go into the production of goods and services are privately owned by individuals or corporations.

Centralisation: When government power is concentrated in one body or person.

Colonial Status: When a country's powers to make decisions for itself on war and peace, political and economic policy are limited and subject to another power. India was a colony under British rule till 1947. The Government of Britain made the political and economic decisions.

Constituent Assembly: An assembly especially created to draw up the Constitution.

Constitutional Monarchy: A democratic state where the head of state is a king or queen with limited powers as defined by the Constitution.

Decentralisation: When government power is distributed between a central body such as the Union Government and its units i.e. the State Governments.

Democratic State: A State where the government is made up of elected representatives. The State allows its citizens certain basic freedoms defined by a constitution. The powers of the Government are defined by the Constitution and the three branches of Government are separated so as to maintain a system of checks and balances. A Democratic State also allows its citizens the right to vote.

Dictatorship: Possession of unlimited power to rule by one man, a political party or a military regime.

Fraternity: Fellowship of man – a sense of brotherhood. A society which does not discriminate on grounds of colour, race, religion, caste, income.

Imperialism: When a country exercises political and economic power over territories not within its borders.

Minorities: People living in India who are not part of the majority group. The term minorities is usually understood as those who are not Hindus which is the religion of the majority of the people living in India. However, the term could be classified on the basis of religion or language or community.

Monarchy: A state where the head of state is an inherited office as that of a king or queen.

Republic: A state where the head of state is an elected office.

Schedule: is part of the article which spells out the details.

Secular: A secular state is one, which acknowledges and respects different religions and cultures within its territory and allows freedom of practice and propagation of religion as a right of the citizen.

Socialist State: Because of the inequitable distribution of wealth, modern Governments are responsible for the welfare of individuals. The Government provides services like free education, free medical care, cheap housing, cheap transport, power and water, subsidised food and opportunities to create an equitable society thus **ensuring human rights for all.** To control the price, it is necessary for the Government to own and control those factors that go into the production of goods.

Sovereign State: A state which has **absolute** power

- to govern its territory the way it desires,
- to organize its own political, economic and social system,
- to enter into agreements with other nations,
- to exchange ambassadors,
- to decide on war or peace.

Theocratic State: A state that believes that absolute power lies with God and therefore the laws of the country must acknowledge religious laws as the basis of all laws.

THE UNION EXECUTIVE

THE PRESIDENT AND THE PRIME MINISTER

WHO DECIDES HOW TO CARRY OUT THE LAWS?

Newspaper headlines:

If you read the newspapers, you will notice that every day decisions are being taken on foreign affairs, trade, how to counter terrorism and crime, and how to counter shortages of food. These headlines above declare a decision made either by the Union Government or by a State Government. **Decisions** and **actions** taken by the ruling Government are referred to as **policies**. The Executive branch of the Government makes policies.

Answer the following questions:

1. Which of the above decisions has been taken by the Union Government?

____

2. Which branch of the Government interprets laws? Select the correct answer.

(a) The Legislature (b) The Executive (c) The Judiciary

____

3. Which branch of the Government makes laws? Select the correct answer.

(a) The Legislature (b) The Executive (c) The Judiciary

____

WE HAVE TWO EXECUTIVES

Some countries have a presidential form of Government. An example is the United States, where executive power is exercised by a President directly elected by the people. In countries like India and England, where there is a **parliamentary form of Government**, real executive power is exercised by the Prime Minister, who is first elected to the Legislature. Parliamentary governments have two heads of State. In England, the Queen is the nominal Head of State. It is a hereditary office. In India, the President is the nominal Head of State.

In a parliamentary form of Government, real power rests with the Parliament. As India is a parliamentary democracy, we have **two** heads of State (refer to page 30).

Heads of State

The **Prime Minister** and the Council of Ministers	**The President** is the formal Head of State.
de facto Head of Government	***de jure*** Head of State

Answer the following questions:

1. Who do you think exercises more power—the President or the Prime Minister?

____

2. What is the need to have two heads of State?

____

____

____

THE PRESIDENT REPRESENTS THE NATION BUT DOES NOT RULE THE NATION

India has adopted a parliamentary form of Government based on the British pattern of Government with the **President** as the **formal** Head of State and the **Prime Minister** as the **effective** Head of State. Dr Ambedkar said at the time of the framing of the Constitution:

'The President represents the nation but does not rule the nation.'

How does the Constitution ensure that the Prime Minister is the de facto Head of State?

The Forty-second Amendment to Article Seventy-four of the Constitution states:

There shall be a Council of Ministers with the Prime Minister at the head to aid and advise the President, who shall, in the exercise of his functions, act in accordance with such advice.

However, the **Forty-fourth Amendment** in 1978 gave the President **the right to advise the Cabinet.** The Amendment implied that the Cabinet was obliged to keep the President informed of major decisions and if the Cabinet failed to do so, it was a violation of Constitutional practice. The Cabinet is free to pay heed to his advice or ignore it.

The President has the right to be heard.

What, then, are the powers of the President? Is he only a titular head?

Answer the following questions:

1. Of the six powers listed under **Powers of the President** on pages 59-61 which power is the President exercising in the following instances?

	Action	Function
1.	The President grants pardon to a woman convicted of murder on compassionate grounds. The sentence of hanging is commuted to life imprisonment.	
2.	The President receives the ambassador from Switzerland, who presents his credentials.	
3.	The President presides over the joint military exercises of the defence forces.	
4.	The President officially appoints the Prime Minister of the country.	
5.	The President does not sign an Ordinary Bill but sends it back to Parliament for reconsideration.	

		Function
6.	The President imposes President's Rule in a State because of the ruling Government's inaction during communal riots.	
7.	The President administers the oath of office to the Chief Justice of India.	
8.	The President delivers his address to both Houses on the opening day of a Parliamentary session.	
9.	In 1998, the President bestowed the Bharat Ratna on M.S. Subbulakshmi, a classical singer in the Carnatic vocal style.	
10.	The President dissolves Parliament.	
11.	The President takes the salute on Republic Day.	
12.	The President can pass a law to curb terrorist activities when Parliament is not in session.	

Know Your Presidents

1. The President of India is

___

2. The Vice President of India is

___

3. How many Presidents has India had since 1950?

___

4. Which two Presidents died while in office?

___

5. Who takes over immediately after a President dies in office?

___

WHO ELECTS THE PRESIDENT?

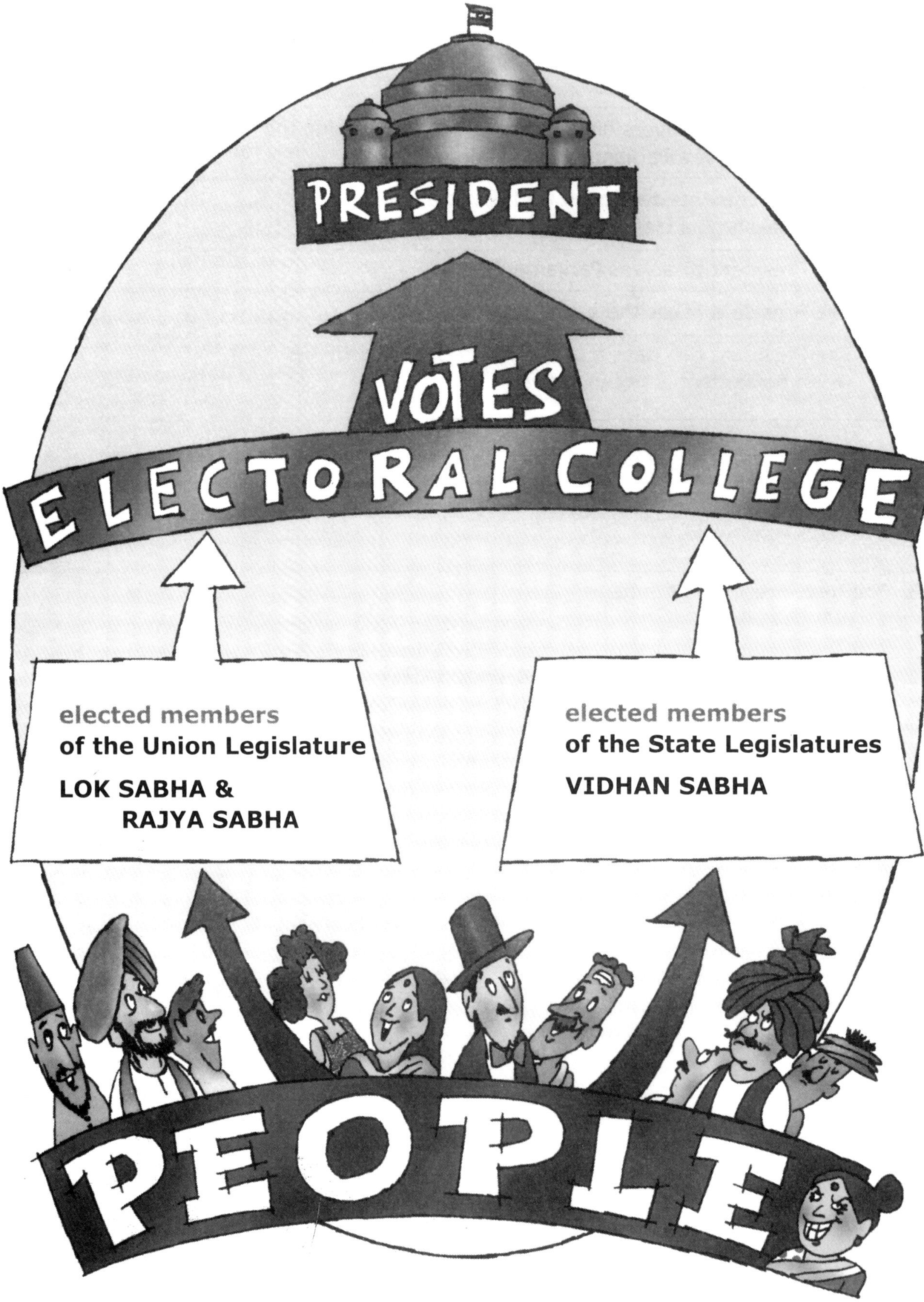

Study the diagram given on page 36 and say whether the following statements are **true** or **false**. Mark with a ✓or ✗.

1.	People vote **directly** for the President.	
2.	People vote **indirectly** for the President.	
3.	Only the elected members of the Union and State Legislatures have a vote in the Electoral College.	
4.	The Electoral College comprises educated people who vote for the President.	
5.	Members nominated by the President to the Rajya Sabha cannot vote.	
6.	Members of the Vidhan Parishad (the Upper House in State Legislatures) cannot vote for the President.	
7.	People vote for the President through their vote for representatives to the Lok Sabha, Rajya Sabha and Vidhan Sabha.	
8.	All members of the State Legislative Assemblies have a right to vote for the President.	
9.	The Electoral College is made up of votes of **elected** members of the Union Legislature—the Lok Sabha and the Rajya Sabha; and votes of the State Vidhan Sabhas.	
10.	The President is nominated by the Electoral College.	
11.	The President is elected by an Electoral College.	

WHO ELECTS THE PRIME MINISTER?

In a parliamentary democracy, people **directly** elect representatives to Parliament. Candidates who contest the elections belong to a political party or are independent candidates. If any one party wins by an **absolute majority**, there is no problem in the appointment of the Prime Minister. The President invites the leader of the party that has won the majority of the seats in Parliament to form the Government and chooses him/her as the Prime Minister. If no party has won by an absolute majority in Parliament, the President calls upon the party that has won the **most seats** to join with other parties and form a Government. However, he/she has to subsequently secure a vote of confidence in the Lok Sabha. In reality, the Prime Minister is chosen by the elected members of a political party and the President officially appoints him.

Answer the following questions:

How is the Prime Minister a lawmaker as well as the chief executive?

WHO ELSE IS PART OF THE EXECUTIVE?

The Prime Minister suggests a list of members he would like to include in the ministry. Thus, the President appoints a Council of Ministers on the advice of the Prime Minister. The Council of Ministers are also Members of Parliament. However, it may happen that the Prime Minister selects as a Minister someone who is not a Member of Parliament but has expertise in a certain field. In that case, the newly appointed Minister must become a Member through a **by-election** within six months of his appointment. A Minister can be a Member of either House of Parliament.

COUNCIL OF MINISTERS

about 60 ministers

CABINET MINISTERS

The Ministers with the most important portfolios—home affairs, defence, finance, foreign affairs, oil and gas, transportation, etc. The Prime Minister **MUST** consult them.

MINISTERS OF STATE

They are below Cabinet Ministers in rank. They **assist Cabinet Ministers** and may or may not hold independent portfolios. The Prime Minister may or may not consult them.

DEPUTY MINISTERS

They assist the Ministers of State and Cabinet Ministers.

Know Your Prime Ministers

1 How many Prime Ministers have we had since Independence?

---

2 Who was the first Prime Minister?

---

3. Why have we had more Prime Ministers than Presidents?

Select the appropriate term from the box below and enter it in Column 2 thus completing the sentence.

the People	Parliament
the Chief Executive of a State Government	the Prime Minister
the Chief Executive of the Union Government	the Finance Minister
the Council of Ministers	the Home Minister
Cabinet Ministers	the President

COLUMN 1	COLUMN 2
1. A Chief Minister is	
2. The Prime Minister is	
3. The Minister in charge of internal affairs, maintaining law and order in the country, is	
4. The oath of office is administered to a Minister by	
5. The annual budget of the Central Government is drawn up by	
6. The Prime Minister is elected by	
7. The Prime Minister is appointed by	
8. The Council of Ministers is appointed by	
9. The salaries and allowances of Ministers are determined by	
10. The most important portfolios are handled by	

WHO DOES WHAT?

Cabinet Ministers are those Ministers who are assigned important **portfolios** to manage. The matter each Minister handles is referred to as a **portfolio. The following table lists** the **54 portfolios of Cabinet Ministers of the Government of the Seventeenth Lok Sabha.**

1. Ministry of Defence	2. Ministry of Home Affairs
3. Ministry of Cooperation	4. Ministry of Road Transport and Highways
5. Ministry of Finance	6. Ministry of Corporate Affairs
7. Ministry of Agriculture and Farmers Welfare	8. Ministry of External Affairs
9. Ministry of Tribal Affairs	10. Ministry of Women and Child Development
11. Ministry of Minority Affairs	12. Ministry of Commerce and Industry
13. Ministry of Consumer Affairs, Food and Public Distribution	14. Ministry of Textiles
15. Ministry of Education	16. Ministry of Skill Development and Entrepreneurship
17. Personnel, Public Grievances and Pensions	18. Ministry of Coal
19. Ministry of Mines	20. Ministry of Micro, Small and Medium Enterprises
21. Ministry of Ports, Shipping and Waterways;	22. Ministry of Ayush
23. Ministry of Social Justice and Empowerment	24. Ministry of Rural Development
25. Ministry of Panchayati Raj	26. Ministry of Civil Aviation
27. Ministry of Steel	28. Minister of Railways
29. Ministry of Communications	30. Ministry of Electronics and Information Technology
31. Ministry of Food Processing Industries	32. Ministry of Jal Shakti
33. Ministry of Earth Sciences	34. Ministry of Power
35. Ministry of New and Renewable Energy	36. Ministry of Petroleum and Natural Gas
37. Ministry of Housing and Urban Affairs	38. Ministry of Health and Family Welfare
39. Ministry of Chemicals and Fertilizers	40. Ministry of Environment, Forest and Climate Change
41. Ministry of Labour and Employment	42. Ministry of Heavy Industries
43. Ministry of Fisheries, Animal Husbandry and Dairying	44. Ministry of Culture
45. Ministry of Tourism	46. Ministry of Development of North Eastern Region
47. Ministry of Information and Broadcasting	48. Ministry of Youth Affairs and Sports
49. Ministry of Statistics and Programme Implementation	50. Ministry of Planning
51. Ministry of Corporate Affairs	52. Ministry of Science and Technology
53. Ministry of Law and Justice	54. Ministry of Parliamentary Affairs

Answer the following questions:

Which Ministry:

1.	provides legal advice to the Government?	
2.	decides that no structures can be erected within 500 yards of beaches in India?	
3.	issues orders to quell riots in a State?	
4.	issues orders to control arbitrary rates imposed on consumers by cable operators?	
5.	censors programmes on television?	
6.	issues orders to change the content of textbooks?	
7.	is in charge of selling shares of Government-owned companies to the private sector?	
8.	decides on taxes to be levied?	
9.	decides that railway fares have to be increased?	
10.	decides not to impose a minimum investment requirement for foreign companies wishing to manufacture cars?	
11.	decides whether we should resume peace talks with a neighbouring country?	
12.	decides to withdraw troops from the country's borders?	
13.	drafts a Bill for women's welfare?	
14.	inquires into the mismanagement of a public limited company?	
15.	decides on the type of equipment to be bought for the army?	

What Do You Think?

Cabinet-rank Ministers play a key role in the policy and decision-making process. They are closest in rank to the Prime Minister.

Do all the 47 Ministries of the Seventeenth Lok Sabha merit Cabinet status?

If you were the Prime Minister, how would you keep your Cabinet down to 12 or 15 Ministers? To which ministries would you give Cabinet status?

1.	
2.	
3.	
4.	
5.	
6.	
7.	
8.	
9.	
10.	
11.	
12.	
13.	
14.	
15.	

THE PRIME MINISTER WEARS MANY MANTLES

The **Prime Minister** is the **leader of the nation**, the actual head of Government in a country which has adopted a parliamentary form of Government. It is his responsibility to form a government in a State when there is a deadlock.

Besides being the leader of the Government, he is also the **leader of the political party in power**.

In a parliamentary form of Government, the Prime Minister is also the **leader of the House in Parliament** and its official spokesman.

He is the **leader of the Cabinet**. The Ministers are expected to follow his advice.

The Prime Minister is assisted in his work by a Council of Ministers. He is the **coordinator of all the Ministries**. He is assisted in this task by the Cabinet Secretariat under the direct charge of the Prime Minister. The Cabinet Secretariat ensures that the President, the Vice President and Ministers are kept informed of the major activities of all Ministries/Departments by means of a monthly summary of their activities.

The Prime Minister is the **link between the President and the Cabinet**. It is the duty of the Prime Minister to convey to the President the decisions of the Council of Ministers relating to administrative matters and proposals for legislation. It is also his responsibility to advice the President to call for President's rule.

What kind of person do you think would make an ideal Prime Minister?

Answer the following questions:

In Box 1 on the left, are the many mantles the Prime Minister wears, showing his responsibilities as a leader. Match these responsibilities with decisions the Prime Minister takes, which are given in Box 2.

BOX 1

1. The Prime Minister is the leader of the nation
2. The Prime Minister is the leader of the political party in power
3. The Prime Minister is the leader of the Cabinet
4. The Prime Minister is the coordinator of all the Ministries
5. The Prime Minister is the link between the President and the Cabinet

BOX 2

a. Decides to invite leaders of other countries to discuss issues on which there are disagreements

b. Decides to attend international meetings to discuss a ban on nuclear weapons

c. Decides in Parliament the action to be taken on controversial issues

d. Advises his Cabinet on steps to be taken in a crisis like the insistence on building a temple at the disputed site in Ayodhya

e. Consults the Ministry for Tourism and the Ministry for Environmental Issues before considering a Bill prohibiting construction of hotels on beaches

f. Consults the Ministry of Defence before agreeing to withdrawal of troops from the border

g. Issues orders to send contingents of the army to quell widespread riots in a State

h. Advises the President on President's Rule because of the inability of any party to form a Government in a State

i. Advises the President on the action to be taken when the country is ravaged by riots

Answers on page 70

WE ARE THE LAWMAKERS AND THE EXECUTORS!

In a parliamentary form of Government, besides the **executive functions** of framing policies to implement the laws and looking after assigned portfolios, the Prime Minister and his Council of Ministers have the following tasks:

- Draw up Bills and initiate them in Parliament = **legislative functions.**
- Control the finances of the Government, prepare the budget, find resources for expenditure, levy taxes and allocate funds for development = **financial functions**.

Which function—executive, legislative, or financial—is the Executive exercising in the following cases?

Action	Function
The Cabinet and Council of Ministers suggest a Bill to prevent terrorism.	
The Cabinet and Ministry of Railways draw up a budget for the railways.	
The Cabinet okays dual citizenship for non-resident Indians.	
The Railway Ministry draws up projects worth Rs 12,000 crore.	
The Cabinet initiates a Bill to make education a Fundamental Right.	
The Defence Ministry decides to withdraw troops from the line of control in Kashmir.	
At the end of the financial year on the last day of February, the Finance Minister presents the budget.	
The Prime Minister and his Council of Ministers initiate a Bill in Parliament for increase in the salaries of Members of Parliament.	
The Prime Minister decides to appoint a Commission of Enquiry to investigate riots in a State.	

WE WORK AS A TEAM!

In a parliamentary form of Government, Ministers are **collectively responsible** to Parliament. It is necessary for the Prime Minister and the Council of Ministers to agree collectively to the policies and decisions made by the Prime Minister and support each other. The blame for the Government's mistakes must be borne by the entire Council. If a **vote of no confidence** is passed against the Government, the Prime Minister and his Council of Ministers have to resign en bloc.

Say What You Think

If you were a Minister, what would you do if you did not agree with the Prime Minister's decision on a policy matter that you know is going to lead to riots and protests?

____

____

What should the Council of Ministers of the Union Government do if a **vote of no confidence** is passed in Parliament against the Government because the Home Minister delayed taking steps to curb riots that led to loss of life and property within a State?

____

____

Members of the Opposition parties condemn and pass a **vote of censure** against a Home Minister for his inaction in quelling riots that led to loss of many lives. Should only the Home Minister take responsibility and resign or should the Prime Minister and the Council of Ministers collectively resign?

____

____

WHO IS RESPONSIBLE?

Besides being collectively responsible for their actions, the Ministers in charge of various departments have **individual responsibility** over their departments and are accountable to Parliament for their mistakes. The Food and Agriculture Minister must take responsibility for food shortages in the country if a problem as severe as starvation deaths or soaring prices of food grains is created.

Answer the following questions:

1. If the Government is questioned and censured in Parliament for shortage of food grains and starvation deaths in some parts of the country, who should resign? Give reasons for your answer.
   - The Prime Minister and his Cabinet
   - The Minister in charge of **consumer affairs, food and public distribution**
2. Who should resign if it is proved in Parliament that one of the Ministers is corrupt? Give reasons for your answer.
   - The Prime Minister and his Cabinet
   - The Minister accused of corruption

Think of a problem that faces the country.

- What is the problem?
- Who has created it? Which Ministry is responsible for this problem?
- What has been done to solve the problem?
- What steps will **you** take to make the Minister accountable for the problem?

EXECUTIVE IN ACTION DURING AN EMERGENCY

Article 352 states: If the President is satisfied that a grave emergency exists whereby the security of India or any State of India is threatened by war or armed rebellion he can make a proclamation declaring a state of general emergency. The President can declare the emergency even before the actual occurrence of war or armed rebellion if he feels there is imminent danger.

What happens when national emergency is imposed?

The **President becomes the sole administrator** of the country and exercises control over the administration of all the States of the Union. The Governors have to take instructions from the President and act in accordance with the directives issued by the President.

Parliament has unrestricted power to make laws regarding any State and regarding any subject even if it is in the State List.

All or some of the **Fundamental Rights can be suspended** or curtailed with the exception of Protection of Life and Personal Liberty. One of the first rights to be suspended in such situations is the Freedom of the Press and other media. In times of war with other countries, freedom to move around the country may be suspended. In times of internal rebellion, foreign correspondents might be restricted in their freedom to photograph and write on politically sensitive areas. Even the right to appeal to the Judiciary for the enforcement of Fundamental Rights may be suspended during an emergency.

Can the President on his own or on the advice of the Prime Minister declare an emergency?

The **Forty-fourth Amendment to the Constitution, 1978,** took care of that.

1 The President cannot declare such an emergency unless the **decision of the Union Cabinet, that is the Prime Minister and his Cabinet, is communicated to him in writing**. It states that the President cannot act on the mere advice of the Prime Minister.

2 The proclamation of emergency has to be approved through a resolution by both Houses of Parliament within 30 days of the date of its issue. If during that period, the

Lok Sabha has been dissolved and composed of newly elected members, the proclamation will be effective for 30 days after the first sitting of the new Lok Sabha provided the Rajya Sabha has in the meantime approved the resolution.

Read the following account of the declaration of national emergency in 1975 and answer the questions that follow:

Until 1974, the Congress Party used to win majority seats in Parliament and form the Government. The mid-seventies were years of unrest. 1974 was a year of high prices, unemployment and lack of essential commodities. Regional parties had emerged in the states and in many states the Congress Party was not in power. There was a nationwide railway strike. Mrs Indira Gandhi, who was the Prime Minister, felt threatened by Jayaprakash Narayan's mass movement in protest. On 5 June 1974, he addressed a mammoth crowd at Gandhi Maidan in Patna. He declared, 'This is a revolution, friends! We are not here merely to see the Vidhan Sabha dissolved. That is only one milestone on our journey. But we have a long way to go ... After 27 years of freedom, people of this country are wracked by hunger, rising prices, corruption ... oppressed by every kind of injustice ... it is a total revolution we want, nothing less!'

On 12 June 1975, the Allahabad High Court held the Prime Minister, Mrs Indira Gandhi, guilty of using illegal practices to win the 1971 elections, thus making her election to the Lok Sabha invalid. Jayaprakash Narayan advised her to resign until her name was cleared by the Supreme Court. Instead, she imposed a general emergency in 1975 claiming there were internal disturbances. She did not consult the Cabinet and took this decision by herself. The emergency regime was marked by mass arrests, suppression of civil rights and censorship of the media. Jayaprakash Narayan was arrested and sent to Chandigarh, where he was kept prisoner in a hospital.

Finally, in January 1977, when Indira Gandhi was confident of winning the elections, she lifted the emergency. Fresh elections were declared and several parties united to form the Janata Party as an opposition in response to her high-handedness. Her party was soundly defeated at the polls. The Janata Party came into power.

Answer the following questions:

1. Originally, the Constitution merely stated that an 'internal disturbance' could call for the President to assume emergency powers when advised by the Prime Minister. What made the Janata Government in 1978 amend the Constitution through the **Forty-fourth Amendment, 1978,** substituting the words 'internal disturbances' with 'armed rebellion'?

2. What made the new Government amend the Constitution, making it compulsory for the Prime Minister to consult the Cabinet before advising the President in writing?

3. When national emergency was announced in 1975, a blank space bordered by a black frame appeared as the editorial of a national newspaper on the front page. Why do you think the editor of the newspaper did that?

4. How would the declaration of national emergency affect your rights as a citizen?

Think About It

Was the proclamation of national emergency in 1975 a step to safeguard the interests of the country or the interests of the Government in power?

Find Out

Find two other instances when national emergency was imposed.

Was it justified? Give reasons for your answer.

PRESIDENT'S RULE—ARTICLE 356: WHAT'S THAT?

Emergency Provisions Regarding States

Article 356 of the Constitution states that if a Governor of a State reports to the President that there has been a breakdown in the functioning of the State Government or if the President is satisfied that a situation has arisen where the governance of a State cannot be carried on according to the laws of the Constitution, the President can assume emergency powers.

- He **dismisses the Vidhan Sabha** or the State Assembly and calls for new elections in the State, imposing President's Rule in the interim period. Total dissolution of the Assembly requires the approval of both Houses of Parliament.
- He keeps the **Legislative Assembly alive in suspended animation**. When law and order has been restored, the Assembly meets again and selects a new leader and a new ministry is formed.
- In such an event, the President and the Union Government assume total control over the legislative, executive and financial functions of the State administration, but not the judicial functions. The proclamation is in operation for a period of six months.

Constitutional Emergency = President's Rule.

What is considered a breakdown in the functioning of a State Government?

It has proved difficult to decide what constitutes a breakdown of a State Government. This has led to the misuse of this Article by various Governments at the Centre to dismiss Governments ruled by Opposition parties in the States. Now the Courts have started interfering and have held the actions of the Central Government as unconstitutional and have revived the Legislatures of the States that were dissolved by the proclamation under Article 356.

Article 356 called upon on ninety or more occasions!

Case Study 1:

Year 1989. The Janata Dal secured the majority in the Legislative Assembly of Karnataka. Due to internal squabbles in the party for power and dissatisfaction over the distribution of ministries, dissidents wrote to the Governor that they had withdrawn their support to the Chief Minister Mr Bommai. Rajiv Gandhi, the Prime Minister, advised the President to dismiss the Government in Karnataka and impose President's Rule.
Mr Bommai was prepared to prove support for his Government but the Governor would not listen. Mr Bommai challenged this decision as unconstitutional, appealing to the Supreme Court. The Court, after examining the case, held that it was an improper exercise of power and hence unconstitutional. It revived the Legislative Assembly for the first time in history.

The Bommai judgement became a landmark for interpretation of the Constitution in the use of Article 356. In doing so, the following principles were laid down by the Court:

(i) The power under Article 356 should be sparingly used. Invoking Article 356 should be the last resort.

(ii) A breakdown of constitutional machinery could be judged by the following criteria. Has there been:

- (a) a large-scale breakdown of law and order,
- (b) gross mismanagement of affairs by a State Government,
- (c) corruption or abuse of power,
- (d) danger to national integration or security of the nation,
- (e) abetting of racial disintegration,
- (f) a claim for independent sovereign status,
- (g) subversion of the Constitution.

On which of the above counts could the Prime Minister have advised the President to impose President's Rule in Gujarat after the March 2002 communal riots?

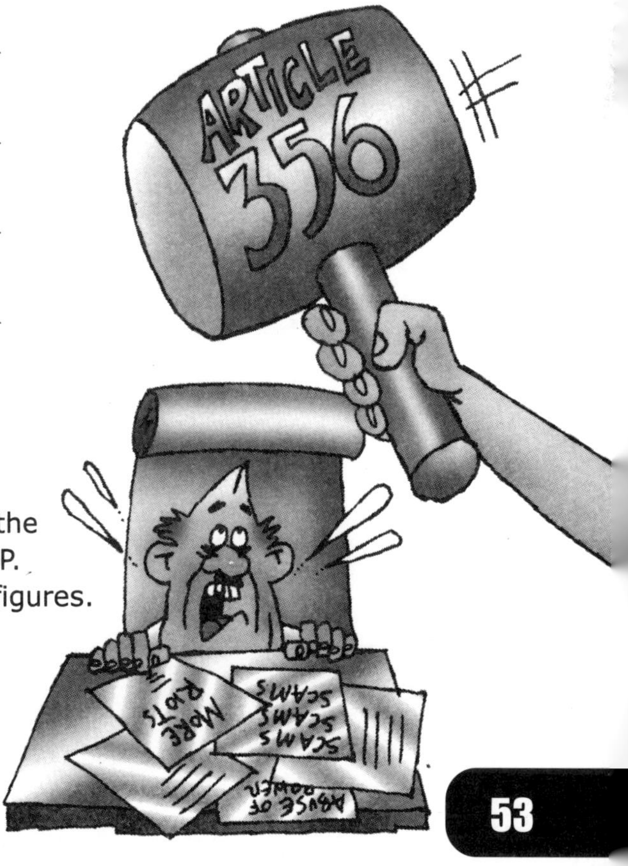

Case Study 2:

Read the next account on the split of the Bhartiya Janata Party (BJP) in Gujarat over the problem of who should be the leader in 1996. There were two rival factions within the BJP. Mr Vaghela and Suresh Mehta were the two controversial figures.

The Times of India, 19 September 1996

'President's Rule was imposed on Gujarat on Thursday following the dismissal of the 18-month-old BJP Government led by Suresh Mehta. The State Assembly has been kept under suspended animation and will be revived as soon as normalcy returns, according to an official spokesman.

The decision for intervention by the centre has been taken on the ground that there was total breakdown of law and order in the State.'

Read the passage above and answer the following questions:

1. In which State was President's Rule imposed?

____

2. What was the reason given for this?

____

3. Which party had formed the Government? Who was the Chief Minister?

____

4. What is meant by '*Assembly has been kept in suspended animation*'?

____

5. Was President's Rule justified in this case?

____

6. Why was the Assembly not totally dissolved?

____

Answer the following questions:

1. How has Article 356 been a threat to the federal structure of India?

____

2. How is a national emergency different from President's Rule?

____

WHICH FORM OF GOVERNMENT—PRESIDENTIAL OR PARLIAMENTARY?

1. Under which system does the system of checks and balances work better? Why?

2. Under which system is there a better chance of the Executive acting in a dictatorial way? Why?

3. Under which system does the Executive have flexibility in appointing a Cabinet of professional people?

4. Under which system is the appointment of a Cabinet more democratic? Why?

5. Under which system is it easier for an electorate to get rid of an Executive who does not listen to the voice of the people? Why and how?

6. Which system do you think is more suitable for India? Give reasons for your answer.

STATE EXECUTIVES—THE GOVERNOR DOES A BALANCING ACT

There are **two Executives** at the State Government level. The **Chief Minister** or the ***Mukhya Mantri*** is the real head while the **Governor** or the ***Rajyapal*** is the formal head. Executive powers and functions of the Chief Minister are limited to the State alone. His legislative function is limited to making laws only on the State List and the Concurrent List.

What is the difference in the appointment of the President and the Governor of a State of the Indian federation?

India is a federation of States. Therefore, the Governor has to act not only in the interests of the State but also of the country. It is his responsibility to protect the Constitution and therefore be vigilant about the laws made in the State Legislature. They must not conflict with the Constitution and Union laws. Keeping this in mind, there is a difference in the way the Governor and the President are appointed.

Does the Governor act as a mouthpiece for the Union Government?

What power has the Governor been armed with to enable him to do the balancing act?

The Governor has several **discretionary powers to use his judgement** to coordinate between the Union and the State. Discretionary powers allow the Governor to act independently of the Council of Ministers. The Governor's role as a representative of the Union Government is very important. If after an election, no one party wins by an absolute majority, the Governor can decide whom to call on to form the coalition government. If there is a breakdown of law and order in a State, the Governor can use his discretionary power to ask for President's Rule. Thus, in certain matters, the Governor **does not act on the advice of the Council of Ministers**.

Should a person active in political life be appointed as Governor?

Generally, an eminent person who has not been too active in political life is recommended for the Governor's post. A person actively involved in political life is not recommended because, as Governor, he/she must not have a bias towards any specific political party. As the Constitutional Head of the State, the Governor needs to remain impartial in his decisions when called upon to settle political disputes in the state.

What Do You Think?

Can Mr XYZ, a member of the Rashtriya Swayamsevak Sangh, a 'kar sevak' at Ayodhya in 1992, be appointed as Governor of Uttar Pradesh by the Government?

FACTS

TYPES OF GOVERNMENT—A COMPARISON

PARLIAMENTARY	PRESIDENTIAL
♦ Two Heads of State: i) The Prime Minister, first **elected** by the people as a Member of Parliament. ii) The President **indirectly elected** through an Electoral College or a monarch holding an inherited office.	♦ One Head of State who is directly elected.
♦ The President or monarch is the **nominal/titular** Head of State.	♦ The President is the **real** Head of State and has more powers.
♦ Policy/decision-making power rests with the Prime Minister and the Council of Ministers directly elected.	♦ Policy/decision-making power rests with the President, who is directly elected.
♦ The Prime Minister and the Council of Ministers are lawmakers and policy/ decision-makers. The Legislature and Executive are not separated—the Executive is also a Member of Parliament.	♦ The President is only the policy-maker. The Legislature is the lawmaker. There is a separation of powers—Executive, Legislature and Judiciary are separate bodies.
♦ The Prime Minister chooses his Council of Ministers from Members elected to Parliament. The Prime Minister and the Council of Ministers are responsible to the Legislature.	♦ The President chooses his Cabinet by appointing people from all fields of life. They are not Members of the Legislature and do not participate in debates. They have to be approved by the Senate.
♦ The President is responsible to the Legislature. The President cannot be removed from office except through impeachment.	♦ The President is responsible to the electorate and the Legislature.
♦ The Prime Minister can be removed through a vote of no confidence in Parliament. The Prime Minister is responsible to the electorate—the people who vote for him.	♦ The President cannot be removed from office except by impeachment.

WHAT ARE THE FUNCTIONS OF THE EXECUTIVE?

Executive Functions

The Prime Minister and the Council of Ministers make **decisions** or **policies** on various subjects, which then have to be implemented through various ministries. Officers of the Civil Service—the Indian Administrative Service—help the Ministers to actually implement their policies. They are bureaucrats or professional administrators.

Legislative Functions

The Ministers are Members of Parliament and therefore part of the Legislature, which is responsible for enacting laws. It is the Ministers who introduce a Government Bill on the floor of the House.

Financial Functions

At the end of every financial year, the Government has to decide what items it will spend its money on. **The Cabinet draws up a plan referred to as the Finance Bill**. The Budget will show how the resources of the Government are allocated among different development projects such as roads, bridges, railways, airports, communication satellites, schools, hospitals, etc. The Government plans for equipment for the defence of our country. Depending on the size of its plan, the Government will accordingly raise revenues by collecting taxes and duties, and raising loans. The financial policy of our Government will vary from year to year according to our needs and is drawn up by the Finance Minister in consultation with the Cabinet Ministers.

WHAT ARE THE PRESIDENT'S POWERS?

1. **The President is the ceremonial Head of State.**

   The President of India takes the salute on Republic Day at the Republic Day Parade. It is the President who administers the oath of office to Members of Parliament. It is the President who bestows the honours—Padma Bhushan and Padma Shri—to citizens in different fields of life. The President receives foreign emissaries—diplomats and ambassadors—who present their credentials to him.

2. **The President's executive powers:**

(i) The President is the Supreme Commander of the combined armed forces. Officially, it is he who declares war or concludes peace treaties. The decision to declare war and make peace, however, rests with the Prime Minister, in consultation with the commanders of the three armed forces.

(ii) The President also has the power to make appointments such as:

- the Prime Minister of India and other Ministers on the advice of the Prime Minister,
- the Chief Justice of India and other judges of the Supreme Court and the High Court,
- the Attorney General,
- the Governors of States.

(iii) The President can also remove from office persons appointed by him.

(iv) It is the President who is officially responsible for the administration of the Union Territories.

3. The President also has some **legislative** powers. The President is an integral part of Parliament, which comprises the President, the Rajya Sabha and the Lok Sabha.

(i) The President opens Parliament and delivers the opening address at the first session of Parliament. This address outlines the internal and foreign policies of the Government.

(ii) The President summons, dissolves or prorogues both Houses of Parliament.

(iii) The President can dissolve the Lok Sabha before its term is over, should there be a vote of no confidence.

(iv) Bills passed by both Houses of Parliament can become laws only after the President signs the Bills. If the President does not sign a Bill and sends it back to Parliament for further consideration, the Houses will reconsider the Bill with the changes and suggestions made by the President. If the Bill is passed again with or without the recommendations and sent to the President a second time, the President cannot withhold his assent.

(v) The President can issue **ordinances**. Ordinances are temporary laws issued when Parliament is not in session. However, these ordinances must be approved by Parliament as soon as it is in session again and the ordinance will cease to be effective six weeks after Parliament meets.

4. The President also exercises limited **financial authority**.

   (i) No Money Bill can be introduced in Parliament without his assent.

   (ii) It is the President who orders the Budget to be placed before Parliament.

5. Exclusive to the President is his **judicial** power to grant pardon, to suspend a death sentence temporarily, or commute a death sentence to a life sentence. The President is the final stage of appeal in criminal cases and only the President has the power to pardon a death sentence. He also has the power to grant pardon in respect of all cases filed under Union and State Laws.

6. The most important powers of the President are his **emergency** powers. In the event of any of the following situations, the President has the power to declare an emergency.

   (i) **General Emergency**: If there is danger of foreign aggression or if the peace and security of the country or any of its states is threatened by an armed rebellion, the President can declare a general emergency. A state of emergency has been proclaimed three times since India's Independence (1947): the first in 1962 during the Chinese aggression; a second declared in 1971 during the Bangladesh War; the third declared in 1975 on grounds of internal disturbances (see page 22).

   (ii) **Financial Emergency**: If the President is satisfied that a situation has arisen whereby the financial stability of the country is threatened, he may, by proclamation, assume emergency powers.

   (iii) **Failure of Constitutional Machinery**: Article 356 of the Constitution states that if a Governor of a State reports to the President that a situation has arisen where the Government of the State cannot be carried on in accordance with the provisions of the Constitution, the President can assume emergency powers. Unfortunately, the interpretation of what the breakdown of Constitutional machinery is, has led to the misuse of this Article by various Governments. Many State Governments have been toppled to suit the ruling party at the Centre using this Article.

- **Jawaharlal Nehru and Lal Bahadur Shastri—**During their tenure as Prime Ministers from 1947 to 1966, President's Rule was invoked ten times.
- **Indira Gandhi—**During her tenure as Prime Minister (1966–1977 and 1980–1984), President's Rule was invoked 41 times.
- **Morarji Desai—**President's Rule was invoked 11 times in 28 months.
- **Charan Singh—**President's Rule was invoked five times in less than six months.
- **Rajiv Gandhi—**President's Rule was invoked eight times in 61 months.
- **Vishwanath Pratap Singh—**President's Rule was invoked twice in 11 months.
- **Chandra Shekhar—**President's Rule was invoked four times in seven months.
- **P. V. Narasimha Rao—**President's Rule was invoked nine times in his first 42 months in office.

PRIME MINISTERS OF INDIA: DURATION IN OFFICE

NAME	TERM OF OFFICE	PARTY THAT FORMED THE GOVERNMENT
Jawaharlal Nehru	15 August 1947 to 27 May 1964	Congress
Gulzari Lal Nanda (caretaker PM)	27 May 1964 to 9 June 1964	Congress
Lal Bahadur Shastri	9 June 1964 to 11 January 1966	Congress
Gulzari Lal Nanda (caretaker PM)	11 January 1966 to 24 January 1966	Congress
Indira Gandhi	24 January 1966 to	Congress
Morarji Desai	24 March 1977 to 27 July 1979	Janata Party
Charan Singh	28 July 1979 to 14 January 1980	Janata Party
Indira Gandhi	14 January 1980 to 31 October 1984	Congress
Rajiv Gandhi	31 October 1984 to 1 December 1989	Congress
V. P. Singh	2 December 1989 to 10 November 1990	Hung Parliament (Janata Dal formed the Government)
Chandra Shekhar	10 November 1990 to 21 June 1991	Hung Parliament (Janata Dal formed the Government)
P. V. Narasimha Rao	21 June 1991 to 16 May 1996	Hung Parliament (Congress formed the Government)
Atal Behari Vajpayee	16 May 1996 to 1 June 1996	BJP
H. D. Deve Gowda	1 June 1996 to 12 April 1997	Hung Parliament (Janata Dal formed the Government with outside support from the Congress)
Inder Kumar Gujral	12 April 1997 to 18 March 1998	Hung Parliament (Janata Dal formed the Government with outside support from the Congress)
Atal Behari Vajpayee	19 March 1998 to 22 May 2004	BJP-led coalition called the National Democratic Alliance.
Dr Manmohan Singh	22 May 2004–May 6, 2014	Congress-led coalition called the United Progressive Alliance (UPA)
Narendra Modi	May 6, 2014	BJP

PRESIDENT AND VICE PRESIDENT

Term of office: The term of a President is five years and the oath of office is administered by the Chief Justice of India. Should the office fall vacant due to death or resignation, the Vice President of India takes over till such time as the new President is elected. The Vice President is **ex officio Chairman** of the Rajya Sabha and has the same functions as the Speaker in the Lok Sabha. He officiates in the absence of the President. The Vice President's **term of office** is also **five** years.

Removal from office: The President can resign from office by addressing his letter of resignation to the Vice President. If the President acts contrary to the provisions of the Constitution or is accused of corruption or of misusing his powers, he can be removed from office through a procedure referred to as **impeachment**. The impeachment charges can be introduced in either House of Parliament and must be passed by a two-third majority in each House of Parliament.

The Vice President can be removed from office for misconduct. His **removal from office** requires a **resolution** passed in the Rajya Sabha by a majority of the members and approved by the Lok Sabha.

Election of a President and a Vice President is by an **electoral college** consisting of members of both Houses of Parliament. He can be re-elected any number of times.

Who is qualified to stand for the office of President or Vice President?

(i) A person has to be a citizen of India

(ii) He/she should be 35 years or more of age

(iii) He/she should not have been declared bankrupt

(iv) He/she should not hold any office in the Union or State Governments and should he/she be holding an office, then he/she must resign from the post before seeking election

(v) A Governor of a State or Minister of the Union or a Vice President can stand for the post of President provided he resigns his post before that.

DEFINITION OF TERMS

Absolute Majority: To win by an absolute majority is to obtain 51 per cent or more of the votes or to win 51 per cent of the seats in the Assembly.

Amendment: A change in the Constitution.

Article: A statement about the precise intentions of the Constitution.

Coalition Government: When several parties join together to form a Government because no one party wins by an absolute majority.

Collective Responsibility: Ministers responsible for decisions as a team.

Disinvestment: Term used to define the selling of Government-owned companies to the private sector.

en bloc: All at the same time.

ex officio: By virtue of his office (because he is the Vice President, he automatically becomes the Chairman of the Rajya Sabha).

Hung Parliament: A Parliament in which no single party or combination of parties contesting together has an absolute majority.

Kitchen Cabinet: An American term for an informal group of advisors to the Executive, sometimes given more importance than the actual Cabinet.

Ministers of State: Rank second in command and are awarded portfolios to assist Cabinet Ministers. Sometimes Ministers of State are awarded portfolios independent of the Cabinet Ministers.

Nominate: Appoint or propose for an election.

Ordinance: A temporary law when Parliament is not in session.

Political Party: A group of people who share the same aims and ideas—the same political philosophy about how a country should be governed. People who agree with the programme being offered by a particular party will vote for that party.

Portfolio: An assignment.

Prorogue: Discontinue sessions of Parliament without dissolving it.

Shadow Cabinet: A would-be Cabinet from the Opposition parties to criticise particular features of Government policy.

Simple Majority: To win by a simple majority is to obtain the largest number of votes.

Titular: In name.

Vidhan Sabha: State Legislative Assembly.

ANSWERS

Answers to '**Which Ministry**' on Page 45

1.	Law, Justice and Company Affairs
2.	Environment and Forests
3.	Home
4.	Information and Broadcasting
5.	Information and Broadcasting
6.	Human Resources Development, Science and Technology
7.	Disinvestment
8.	Finance
9.	Railways
10.	Commerce and Industry
11.	Foreign Affairs
12.	Defence
13.	Social Justice and Empowerment
14.	Law, Justice and Company Affairs
15.	Defence

Answers to questions on page 48.

1. 1–a, b
2. 2–c
3. 3–d, h
4. 4–e, f
5. 5–h, i

THE LEGISLATURE

WHAT IS A GOVERNMENT?

People form governments. To govern is to rule. To rule is to manage a country. **People** living within a territory surrender individual freedom to form a State and give **authority** to a body of people: the **Government.**

Equitable = fair & just

WHAT DO PEOPLE EXPECT OF A GOVERNMENT?

EXPECTATIONS	ACTIONS
• Protect freedom • Protect rights • Provide law and order and security in people's lives • Protect people from civil strife and war • Provide basic services like free education, free medical care, cheap housing, cheap public transport, power and water, subsidised food, and equal opportunities • Ensure benefits and costs to society are distributed fairly so as to create a just and equitable society	1. Enact equitable laws 2. Implement laws by making policies and taking decisions that serve the interest of all 3. Interpret laws and settle disputes peacefully and equitably

THE DECISION MAKING POWER OF THE GOVERNMENT IS DIVIDED BETWEEN:

The Legislature, The Executive, & The Judiciary

Fill in the blanks in the following sentences and complete the definitions and functions of the Government:

1. A **GOVERNMENT** is a body of people that exercises ....to enact laws, implement them and enforce the same laws so as to...
2. Name the following branches of Government:
   i) The body that enacts laws is the..
   ii) The body that makes policy decisions and implements policies for the management of the country's affairs is the..
   iii) The body that decides whether the law is compatible with the Constitution and settles disputes peacefully and equitably is the ....

WHY DO WE NEED A GOVERNMENT?

Everyone has a right to life, liberty, and property. Everyone is born with these rights. These rights are called **natural rights**. They are **fundamental** to human nature – all persons have these rights because they are human beings.

How do you protect these Rights?

John Locke, the famous English philosopher wrote in his book *Two Treatises of Civil Government* (1690) that the main **purpose of government was to protect natural rights.**

Living in a state of nature, people might feel free to do anything they want to do. John Locke reasoned that people should agree with one another to give up some of their freedom in exchange for protection of their natural rights. He called this agreement a **Social Contract.**

A social contract is an agreement people make among themselves to give up some of their freedom to create a **government** to **rule** them and **protect their natural rights.** They need a **government:** a body with **authority** to make laws to protect their rights. In return, people consent to obey the laws created by that government.

How will you solve this problem?

Imagine a situation where your class goes on a picnic to an island off the coast of Mumbai. Because of a severe storm you are stranded on the island for an indefinite period. There is no habitation on the island. There are no means of communication with the outside world except the launch you travelled on. Your cell phone does not pick up signals. The boat cannot go back to secure help till the storm abates. You have some food for four days at the most. What action will you take for an indefinite stay on the island?

1. What rights do you think each child is entitled to during the stay on the island?
2. How will you decide who makes the decisions on behalf of the whole class?
3. What decisions will that person/group make to ensure the Rights of every individual are respected?
4. Explain the steps you will take to maintain harmony and ensure that everyone's rights are respected.

AN INEFFECTIVE GOVERNMENT IS AS GOOD AS NO GOVERNMENT

How can the absence of effective authority endanger lives, liberty, and property?

Read the following account:

'The devil seems to have unleashed a reign of terror in our town. Rioters are out in the streets with guns and knives and crowbars. In every neighbourhood there are fires burning as a result of arson and explosions of crudely made bombs. The alleys are strewn with mutilated bodies. Once blood is spilled, killing comes easy.

The citizens are afraid of going outdoors. They look on at the carnage from behind drawn curtains.

The police claim they are helpless and cannot take any action. Some citizens appeal to the Government. The Government watches, makes a feeble attempt to stop the killings but pleads helplessness.

After the riots no action is taken against the rioters. A few newspapers condemn the killings and Government inaction but their censure drowns in the silence of the majority.'

CAN YOU TELL?

1. What problems arose in this town because there was no **effective authority**?
2. Why was there no authority?
3. What Rights did the citizen lose in this turmoil?
4. How might the Government have dealt with this problem?
5. Has such a problem happened in your town because of the absence of authority? Discuss similar situations in other countries.
6. Write a letter to the editor of a newspaper commenting on the Government's inaction with reference to the above or any other problem where there has been no effective authority. (Refer to the sample letter for the layout.)

   Notice that the editor has been addressed as 'Sir', not 'Dear Sir'.

A Sample Letter

x xxxxxxxxxxxx,
xx xxxxxxxxxx xxxx,
Orissa
5 January, 1988

The Editor,
Times of India,
Bori Bunder,
Bombay 400 001

Sir,

What saddens me most is the indifference adopted by our Government towards scientists and innovators. As Dr. Bhatt, the renowned scientist, did not get any encouragement for his scientific discovery in India he left for the United States. There he won international acclaim and the Indian Government was quick to claim him as their own. The Government should not complain about the brain drain! They deserve it!

Yours sincerely,
A.K. Das

WHY THREE BRANCHES OF GOVERNMENT?

It is necessary to divide the decision making power of Government between three separate branches of Government: the **legislature, the executive, and the judiciary.** The Constitution confers specific powers to each of these bodies so **they can use this power to check the misuse of power by any of the other branches.**
A system of **checks and balances** prevents the concentration of power in a small group of politicians, who otherwise could make arbitrary laws or decisions.

UNION GOVERNMENT
represents ALL the States of the Union of India

LEGISLATURE = PARLIAMENT	**EXECUTIVE**	**JUDICIARY**
RAJYA SABHA & LOK SABHA make laws	PRESIDENT & THE PRIME MINISTER & COUNCIL OF MINISTERS implement laws	SUPREME COURT JUDGES settle disputes according to laws

The Constitution has provided for many such checks and balances in our system of Government.

A system of Government where one authority checks the power of the other—

Rajya Sabha ⇄ Lok Sabha

The Legislature ⇄ Prime Minister

President ⇄ The Legislature

The Judiciary ⇄ The Legislature

The Judiciary ⇄ State Governments

HOW DOES IT WORK?

THE JUDICIARY

THE EXECUTIVE = The President, Prime Minister, and Council of Ministers

THE LEGISLATURE = Members of Parliament

PARLIAMENT : THE UNION LEGISLATURE

Article 79 of the Constitution states:

There shall be a Parliament for the Union, which shall consist of the President and two Houses to be known as The Council of States and The House of the People.

PARLIAMENT is the Union Legislature, the law making body for the whole country. The Union Government represents all the States of the Union of India. The word Parliament originates from the French word *parler* – to speak. *Parley* is a conference for debating points in dispute. Thus, Parliament is a place where debates are held on various issues and then decisions are unanimously passed as laws.

PARLIAMENT

Two Houses = Bicameral system
Upper House — Rajya Sabha
Lower House — Lok Sabha

DO YOU KNOW WHAT LEGISLATURES OF OTHER COUNTRIES ARE KNOWN AS?

Country	Bicameral System	Legislature: Term used	Upper House	Lower House
India	✓	Parliament	Rajya Sabha	Lok Sabha
USA	✓	Congress	Senate	House of Representatives
United Kingdom	✓	Parliament	House of Lords	House of Commons
Russia	✓	Federal Assembly	Federation Council	The State Duma
Italy	✓	Parlamento	Senato della Repubblica Senate	Camera dei Deputati Chamber of Deputies
France	✓	Le Parlement	Le Sénat Senate	L'Assemblee Nationale National Assembly
Federal Republic of Germany	✓	Parliament	Bundesrat Federal Council	Bundestag Federal Assembly
Pakistan	✓	Federal Legislature	Senate	National Assembly
Bangladesh	✗	Parliament Bangladesh *Jatiya Sansad*	✗	*The Jatiya Sansad* The National Assembly
Japan	✓	The National Diet	House of Councillors	House of Representatives

HOW ARE MEMBERS OF PARLIAMENT ELECTED?

PARLIAMENT

MEMBERS OF PARLIAMENT

RAJYA SABHA	LOK SABHA
MAXIMUM **250 MEMBERS** **238** MEMBERS **INDIRECTLY** ELECTED BY STATE LEGISLATIVE ASSEMBLIES 12 MEMBERS NOMINATED BY THE PRESIDENT	MAXIMUM **550 MEMBERS** **530** MEMBERS **DIRECTLY** ELECTED BY PEOPLE TO REPRESENT 28 STATES on the basis of universal adult suffrage and voting by secret ballot 20 MEMBERS REPRESENT 8 UNION TERRITORIES 2 MEMBERS NOMINATED BY THE PRESIDENT

State whether the statements below about India's parliamentary elections are correct or incorrect. Indicate the ones that are true with a ✓ and the ones that are false with a ✗ :

- ☐ Anybody who is an Indian citizen and at least 18 years of age can vote in elections to Parliament.
- ☐ Anybody who is an Indian citizen and at least 18 years of age can vote in elections to the Rajya Sabha.
- ☐ Only those who can read and write can vote for elections to Parliament.
- ☐ A voter has to inform the Electoral Commission who he or she has voted for.
- ☐ Members to the Rajya Sabha are elected by members of State Legislative Assemblies.
- ☐ Amitabh Bachchan, the actor, can become a member of the Rajya Sabha without being elected.
- ☐ Alok Mitra, a registered voter in Kolkata, can stand for election to the Lok Sabha from one of the constituencies in Maharashtra.
- ☐ Ms Nandita Sen has been a member of the Rajya Sabha for 10 years.
- ☐ As the Rajya Sabha is a permanent House it can never be dissolved.

---

[1]Three Bills passed in July/August 2000 created three new states – Uttarakhand, Chhattisgarh, and Jharkhand.

WHO DECIDES ON THE MAGIC NUMBER OF 550 MEMBERS IN THE LOK SABHA?

550 MEMBERS REPRESENT 1.4 BILLION PEOPLE

What is the ratio of people to one representative?

As a democratic state, people have an equal voice in an election to Parliament. The states of the Indian Federation are represented in Parliament **in proportion to their population.**

Parliament decides from time to time, as and when the population increases or decreases, what the number of members should be. A Delimitation Commission is set up specifically for this purpose. It determines the size and number of constituencies according to the size of the population.

Each state is divided into **constituencies – areas with equal units of population.** The **ratio** between the number of representatives and the population is the **same** for all states. Each constituency sends **one** representative to the Lok Sabha. In this way a state with a larger population has more representatives to the Union Government than states with smaller populations.

CAN YOU TELL?

Refer to the table on the next page and name the three states that have the largest number of constituencies? List them in order of their size.

1. Which state has the most representatives to Parliament?
2. How will this affect voting when laws are being passed in Parliament?
3. Which states have the least number of constituencies? Why?
4. Why will the number of representatives from each state not be a constant figure from election to election?

THINK ABOUT

1. Will the number of constituencies remain the same when a new state is carved out of the old one?
2. How will the constituencies of the recently created state of Uttaranchal, carved out from Uttar Pradesh, be organised?

TABLE PATTERN OF CONSTITUENCIES

Number of representatives from each state:

	STATES	LOK SABHA	RAJYA SABHA
1	Andhra Pradesh	25	11
2	Arunachal Pradesh	2	1
3	Assam	14	7
4	Bihar	40	16
5	Chhattisgarh	11	5
6	Goa	2	1
7	Gujarat	26	11
8	Haryana	10	5
9	Himachal Pradesh	4	3
10	Jammu and Kashmir	5	4
11	Jharkhand	14	6
12	Karnataka	28	12
13	Kerala	20	9
14	Madhya Pradesh	29	11
15	Maharashtra	48	19
16	Manipur	2	1
17	Meghalaya	2	1
18	Mizoram	1	1
19	Nagaland	1	1
20	Odisha	21	10
21	Punjab	13	7
22	Rajasthan	25	10
23	Sikkim	1	1
24	Tamil Nadu	39	18
25	Telangana	17	7
26	Tripura	2	1
27	Uttar Pradesh	79	31
28	Uttarakhand	5	3
29	West Bengal	42	16
	TOTAL	**543**	**245**

It is through the election process to Parliament that we see democracy in action. The Election Commission, a body separate from the government, controls the process of elections. It prepares, maintains, and updates the Electoral roll. It sets the date for elections and plans, supervises and directs the elections. The President appoints the Chief Election Commissioner. The Executive cannot interfere with the work of the Election Commission.

WHO HAS MORE POWER: RAJYA SABHA OR LOK SABHA?

Mark a ✓ against the true statements and a ✗ against the false statements.

☐ In 1975, Mrs Gandhi declared an Emergency without the knowledge of the President.

☐ All the members in the Lok Sabha are elected and the members in the Rajya Sabha are nominated.

☐ The election of all the members in the Rajya Sabha is an indirect election.

☐ The Rajya Sabha can declare that a subject like education is of national importance and, therefore, should be a subject on the Union List.

☐ Only the Lok Sabha has the power to introduce a Money Bill.

☐ If the Rajya Sabha does not pass the Finance Bill, it cannot be passed.

☐ Members of the Rajya Sabha can pass a vote of no confidence in the government of the ruling party.

☐ An ordinary Bill to introduce free education for all girl children needs to be passed only in the Rajya Sabha.

☐ The Rajya Sabha can suggest amendments on a Money Bill.

☐ The Lok Sabha does not have to accept the amendments on a Money Bill made by the Rajya Sabha.

CAN YOU TELL?

1. If the Upper House passes an ordinary Bill and the Lower House does not pass the same Bill there will be a joint session of the two Houses in Parliament. In all probability, the Lower House will win. Why?
2. Why is it that the Union Executive can be forced to resign through a vote of no confidence in the Lok Sabha only?
3. If decision making power were to be weighed, in whose favour would the scales tilt?
4. Name three subjects on which Parliament can pass an ordinary Bill.
5. Name two ways in which the Rajya Sabha **checks the power** of the Lok Sabha.

WHAT CAN PARLIAMENT DO?

Facts-at-the-Back

Mark a tick ✓ against the statement that describes what the legislature can do and a cross ✗ against the statement which describes what it is not empowered to do.

Parliament has the power to:	✓ or ✗
1. Pass a Bill creating a new state.	
2. Pass a vote of no confidence against the Government because the country's finances are in a critical state.	
3. Elect the Vice President of India.	
4. Question ministers on appropriate measures not taken in the event of a railway accident.	
5. Raise taxes on imported consumer goods.	
6. Put to vote a cut in judges' salaries.	
7. Nominate the President.	
8. Make laws to regulate the conduct of elections in the country.	
9. Pass a resolution to remove a Supreme Court judge from office.	
10. Organise and direct elections for the Lok Sabha.	

I INSIDE PARLIAMENT

HOW LAWS ARE MADE IN PARLIAMENT

A Bill goes through several stages before it is passed.

If a Bill is being introduced by the government in power, the Ministry concerned draws up the Bill and sends it to the Law Ministry to check whether it conforms to the Articles of the Constitution. After reviewing the Bill, the Law Ministry sends it to the Cabinet and the Minister in Charge introduces it in Parliament.

If any Member of Parliament, other than a Minister, introduces the Bill on the floor of the House, it is a **private member's Bill.** Thirty days notice has to be given before the Bill can be introduced on the floor of the House.

Motion is a proposal for making a law.

First Reading: The mover does not discuss the Bill in detail but explains why it has been initiated, and what the objectives to be achieved through the passing of this Bill are. An ordinary Bill can be introduced in either House of Parliament. **A Money Bill can be introduced ONLY in the Lok Sabha.**

After the House accepts the motion, a **resolution,** which is **a formal declaration for introducing a Bill, is passed.** If the motion is opposed by a majority of the members of the House, the Bill is said to have died. After the resolution is passed, **a draft of the proposed law** i.e., a **Bill**, is drawn up for debate in Parliament.

When a resolution is passed a Bill is admitted for discussion in the Parliament.

Second Reading: At this stage various steps could be taken:

The Discussion Stage

- The Bill might be referred to a special committee of the House or a Joint Committee of both Houses for discussion. The committee studies the proposed Bill, then it sends to the House where the Bill originated.
- The Bill can be directly discussed on the floor of the House. The Bill is discussed in detail, and amendments are proposed, accepted, or rejected by the House. Each clause is voted upon separately.

Third Reading:

The debate is a discussion in support of the Bill or against it. At the end of the debate, a vote is taken and if it is passed, it is then referred to the second House for debate and discussion.

Second Opinion:
Referred to the Second House

The same procedure is followed in the second House.
After the debate in both Houses, the **Bill** is passed by both Houses of Parliament. An ordinary Bill has to be passed in both Houses.

Final Stage:
President's Signature

The Bill is then sent to the President. He can make suggestions and amendments but Parliament does not have to accept them. The President can refuse to sign the Bill and send it back to Parliament. But if Parliament passes the Bill for a second time then the President cannot withhold his assent. When the President signs the Bill it becomes a **LAW,**
which is the same as an **ACT**

CAN YOU TELL?

Trade Union (Amendment) Bill, 2000 introduced in Parliament.

Below are ten jumbled paragraphs, which outline the process of passage of this Bill. Rearrange the paragraphs so as to trace the Bill from its Introduction stage to the Final stage when it will be passed by both Houses, and becomes an **ACT**.

1. A resolution is passed to admit the Bill for discussion.
2. The Bill is referred to the President of India. Write what happens next if he does not sign it?
3. The Bill is referred to the Lower House and is passed unanimously.
4. The Bill is passed in the Upper House.
5. The Bill is read clause by clause and each clause is voted upon.
6. The Bill is referred to a subcommittee. The committee makes some changes and sends the Bill back to the House for discussion.
7. The Bill is referred to the Lower House.
8. The Bill is then presented to the House to seek a vote.
9. The Labour Minister Dr. XYZ introduces a Bill in the Rajya Sabha today to further amend the Trade Unions Act, 1926. The Trade Union (Amendment) Bill, 2000 aims at reducing the number of trade unions. The Bill proposes that it would require at least 10% or 100 workers engaged or employed in an establishment or industry to form a trade union. At no event can a union be registered without a minimum strength of 7 members.
10. The Legislative Department in the Ministry of Law, Justice and Company Affairs processes the legislation for introduction in the Houses of Parliament.

Now,
in the table below,
trace the four stages of
passage of a Bill:

Stage 1: Introduction	
Stage 2:	
Stage 3:	
Final Stage:	

CAN YOU TELL?

What kind of a Bill is this?

WHO IS A REFEREE IN PARLIAMENT?

Debate implies that there has to be a person to conduct, moderate, and regulate the debate. The presiding officers in the Lok Sabha are referred to as **THE SPEAKER** and **THE DEPUTY SPEAKER**. The Speaker is the spokesman in Parliament and acts as the 'eyes and ears' of all the parliamentarians. The Speaker and the Deputy Speaker are elected unanimously by **all** the Parties in the House. When the Lok Sabha is dissolved, the Speaker continues in office until a new Speaker is elected when the new Lok Sabha meets. The presiding officer of the Rajya Sabha is the Vice President of India.

THE FUNCTIONS OF A SPEAKER

Presides over Meetings in the House

- draws up the agenda for discussion and decides which questions should be debated first.
- interprets the rules and procedure for parliamentary meetings.
- adjourns the House if it lacks a quorum. There must be a minimum number of members present to hold the debate in Parliament.
- presides over joint sessions of Parliament.
- is the intermediary between the President and Parliament.

Maintains Order and Discipline

- he allows a member to speak.
- ensures all comments and remarks are addressed to the Speaker. Members cannot address remarks to each other.
- decides whether an objection raised by a Member of Parliament should be sustained or not.
- orders a member to stop speaking and let another member speak.
- asks a member to leave the House - expel a member for the day or whole session - for offensive behaviour in the house.

Makes decisions

- decides which question should be admitted for debate, and if it is against public interest, he can disallow the question.
- examines the Bill to ascertain whether it is a Money Bill or an ordinary Bill.
- has the casting vote, should there be a tie when voting on a Bill in the Lok Sabha.
- has the casting vote, should there be a tie in the votes at a joint sitting of Parliament.

RECOGNISING PARLIAMENTARY LANGUAGE

CAN YOU TELL?

Match these answers to explain the terms in the left-hand column of the table.

1. A Member of Parliament leaves his political party to join another political party.
2. A tie in voting.
3. A vote given to the Speaker if there is a tie in the vote on a Bill in the Lok Sabha or in a joint session of Parliament.
4. Allow a member to speak.
5. An objection raised by an MP in response to a comment.
6. Discontinue meetings of Parliament without dissolving it.
7. Member asks if he can speak.
8. A member is ordered by the Speaker to discontinue his speech and allow another member to speak.
9. Order Parliament to meet.
10. Plan topics for discussion at a meeting.
11. Postpone the debate for another session.
12. The minimum number of members required to hold a meeting, otherwise the meeting is not valid.

1. Casting vote	
2. Yield to the floor	
3. Draw up the agenda	
4. Point of order	
5. A quorum	
6. Adjourn the meeting	
7. Recognise member on the floor of the House	
8. Permission of the chair	
9. Cross the floor	
10. Summon Parliament	
11. Prorogue the session	
12. Deadlock	

WHO ARE THE VIPs IN PARLIAMENT?

Prime Minister and Council of Ministers

INDIA HAS ADOPTED A PARLIAMENTARY FORM OF GOVERNMENT

The Executive: The Prime Minister and the Council of Ministers are also part of Parliament, and not separate from it as in a Presidential form of Government. They exercise legislative and executive functions. Candidates are first elected as Members of Parliament – The Legislature. They become ministers only after the elections. The President asks the party that has won a majority or most of the 550 seats in Parliament to form the EXECUTIVE BRANCH of the Government – the body that will frame policies and initiate laws.

THE MPs OF THE PEOPLE'S PARTY ELECTED TO PARLIAMENT

The leader of the party that has the second largest number of members in Parliament is chosen as the **LEADER OF THE OPPOSITION.**

CAN YOU TELL?

1. Who is the present Prime Minister of India?
2. Who is the Leader of the Opposition in the present government?
3. Name all the Prime Ministers since 1947 and state their term of office.
4. What is the difference between a Prime Minister and a Chief Minister?

HOW DOES THE LEGISLATURE EXERCISE CONTROL OVER EXECUTIVE ACTIONS?

The ways in which the Legislature makes ministers responsible for their actions are:

The Minister announces a hike in the price of petroleum and petro-products. The price of petrol will again rise. There will be a steep increase in the price of a gas cylinder. Kerosene prices will go up. The cost of living will rise.

How will the legislators explain this rise in prices to people in their constituencies?

How will legislators demand an explanation from the minister on whether the rise in prices is justified?

Interpellation: The right to ask questions is referred to as **interpellation.** Every day during a Parliament session, one hour is set aside to ask ministers questions about matters affecting the day-to-day life of the citizens for which ministers are collectively answerable to the people. Questions are asked to elicit information, to ensure accountability.

Answers to questions have to be precise and accurate. The minister/ministers concerned cannot mislead the public. If it is later found that the information is inaccurate or incorrect, the minister has to make a statement in the House correcting the previous answer. Where ministers feel that they cannot supply complete and accurate information at the moment, they can ask for more time.

LOK SABHA[2]

LIST OF BUSINESS
Tuesday, August1, 2000/Sravana 10, 1922 (*Saka*) 11 A.M.

QUESTIONS

1. QUESTIONS entered in separate list to be asked and answers given.

A PART OF THE AGENDA OF A PARLIAMENTARY SESSION

Find Out

Search for news on questions asked in Parliament during the next parliamentary session. Make a scrapbook of the questions asked during one session of Parliament.

[2]Refer to website: parliamentofindia.nic.in

Think About

Pretend you are a Member of Parliament. Think of three current issues you are not happy about and ask questions to a minister/ministers.

1. --

2. --

3. --

Vote of No Confidence: If the government makes a law that is not in line with the Constitution, the Opposition members can call for a debate on the issue and a vote is taken. If the result of the debate is a **vote of no confidence**, the Prime Minister and his Council of Ministers have to resign collectively and another government will have to be formed either by the other members in Parliament or through fresh elections.

An adjournment motion: Another method of censuring the government is through an adjournment motion.

A railway accident has taken place in Bihar. Hundreds of people have died. How did the accident take place? Has there been neglect on the part of the Railway Ministry? All these issues need to be discussed immediately.

Members of Parliament ask for the discussion of topics listed in the agenda for the day to be postponed for discussion later in order to debate the issue raised in the motion. These adjournment motions are usually passed in order to discuss critical issues or serious incidents like a communal riot or a railway accident. The Opposition members may refuse to continue the debate condemning government failure in taking preventive measures.

Rejection of a Bill: One of the government members might introduce a Bill to change the structure of the Constitution. Such a law may not be acceptable to other MPs. The Opposition members then refuse to pass the Bill in Parliament, and through their rejection of the Bill show their disapproval of government actions. The Opposition has to act as the watchdog for the country.

WHO PAYS FOR ALL THIS?

PRIVILEGES OF MEMBERS OF PARLIAMENT

Other privileges include:
- the right to free speech in Parliament.
- cannot be prosecuted for any statements made in Parliament and reported by the Press.
- A Member of Parliament cannot be placed under arrest when Parliament is in session, and if the charge is a serious criminal charge like murder, then the permission of the Chairman of the House has to be sought.

- a monthly salary
- a daily allowance
- constituency allowance
- office expense allowance
- allowance for expenses on stationery
- travelling allowance
- free railway pass to travel anywhere in India
- housing facilities
- medical facilities
- income tax relief
- foreign exchange allowance
- diplomatic passport
- pension for life
- 3 telephones installed, one at the office, at home and one at the constituency
- 50,000 free telephone calls a year

SHOULD YOU NOT DEMAND GOOD VALUE FOR YOUR MONEY?

1. How often does your legislator (MP) visit his/her constituency?
2. What specific problems does your constituency have?
3. What do you expect your representative to do?
4. What code of conduct do you expect from your MPs? Suggest some rules that they should follow.
5. Collect information about different Members of Parliament. Read newspapers and journals. Watch TV news channels.
   i) If you were to award a prize for the best MP, whom would you name?
   ii) Draw up a list of personal qualities and accomplishments to use as a yardstick to judge the best MP.

How do we as voters make MPs responsible to the electorate?

When we invest money we expect profits, interest, or dividends.

When we invest in human resources we expect services rendered with honesty and sincerity not misuse of power.

HOW ARE STATE LEGISLATURES ORGANISED?

29 States = 29 Legislatures = 29 Vidhan Sabhas

The Legislative Assembly of a state is referred to as **The Vidhan Sabha.**

LEGISLATIVE ASSEMBLY

VIDHAN SABHA

MLAs

NOT MORE THAN 500 MEMBERS
NOT LESS THAN 60 MEMBERS

The population of a state determines the number of members in each State Legislative Assembly. Each state is divided into territorial constituencies. The states that are larger in area have more constituencies than the smaller states. One member is elected from each constituency.

FIND OUT

1. What is the size of the Legislative Assemblies in Goa, Sikkim, and Mizoram?
2. Compare it with the size of the Legislative Assemblies in Maharashtra, Uttar Pradesh, and Madhya Pradesh.
3. Name the states that have a second chamber — the Vidhan Parishad.

CAN YOU TELL?

Do State Legislative Assemblies have the same powers as the Union Parliament?

i) How many subjects on the state List can the Vidhan Sabha make laws on? Compare it to the number of subjects on the Union List.
ii) If a state law contradicts a Union law, which law will prevail?

WHY HAVE TWO HOUSES IN PARLIAMENT?

1. In a Federal State, the second chamber of Parliament represents the will of the states that form the federation, as members to the Upper House are elected by the Legislatures of the federating states.
2. Through nominations to the Upper House, people from different disciplines and professions are also represented in Parliament. Thus, movie stars, musicians, doctors, social activists, professors, and scientists also participate in the law making process.The Upper House acts as a check on laws being hastily passed. If a law has been introduced and approved in the Lower House, it has to be sent to the Upper House for consideration. The time delay is a period for reflection on the merits and demerits of the Bill.
3. The second chamber also acts as a check on the power of the Lower House. A Bill may be passed in the Lower House by a Government determined to introduce an unpopular law. Because it has the majority in the Lok Sabha the Bill would be passed. However, if it has to be sent for reconsideration to the Upper House, the chances are that an unpopular Bill might not be passed. It, thus, acts as a check on the rule of the majority.

SOME FACTS ABOUT PARLIAMENT

RAJYA SABHA:	
Members are indirectly elected	by elected members of State Legislative Assemblies.
The seats allotted to the states	are in proportion to their population. For example in Maharashtra, the State Assembly will elect 19 members to the Rajya Sabha, whereas the Kerala State Assembly will elect only 9 members to the Rajya Sabha.
Nominated Members:	The President nominates 12 members with special knowledge or practical experience in literature, science, art, and social service – people like artists, writers, actors, scientists, and social activists.
Eligibility for membership to the Rajya Sabha:	The candidate must be a registered voter in the state he or she is representing.
Term of the Rajya Sabha:	The Rajya Sabha is a permanent body. It cannot be dissolved. The term of office for each member is 6 years. 1/3 of the members retire every 2 years and new members are elected.

LOK SABHA:	
Members directly elected	by people on the basis of Universal Adult Franchise from single member constituencies. Elections are held every 5 years.
Who is eligible to stand for elections as representative?	• Must be a citizen of India. • Must not be less than 25 years of age. • Must not be employed by any government-owned company, which is profit motivated. Thus, a professor of a government university can stand for election, but a person employed by, say, the Steel Authority of India has to resign his job and then stand for election. • Must be legally free of debts. A person cannot stand for election if he/she is bankrupt. • Must be of sound mind. • Must not be convicted of a crime. • The candidate need not be a resident of the state he represents.
Composition of the Lok Sabha:	All the states of the Union are represented in the Lok Sabha in proportion to their population. The ratio between the number of representatives and the population is the same for all states. This is achieved by dividing the country into units called constituencies, each with approximately equal units of population. Each constituency elects a member to represent them in the Parliament. If the Anglo-Indian community has not been represented through an election, the President has the power to nominate not more than two members of that community to the House of the People. Seats are also reserved for Scheduled Castes and Tribes in the House of the People. Scheduled Castes are the underprivileged as defined by the Constitution. Each state will be allowed reserved seats in proportion to the population of the Scheduled Castes and Tribes in that state. In 1998, of the 543 seats, 120 seats were reserved for Scheduled Castes and Tribes.
Term of the Lok Sabha:	5 years, unless the government is voted out of power within that period through a no confidence motion.

THE POWERS OF THE RAJYA SABHA COMPARED WITH THAT OF THE LOK SABHA:-

RAJYA SABHA	LOK SABHA
1. Members of the Rajya Sabha are entitled to vote for the President. 2. When the Lok Sabha is not in session the Rajya Sabha has to approve the declaration of an Emergency by the President. 3. Rajya Sabha has the power to declare any subject on the State List as a subject of national importance and move the subject to the Union List. 4. Members of the Rajya Sabha can vote in a debate for the removal of any Supreme Court or State High Court judge. 5. Members of the Rajya Sabha have equal powers as those of the Lok Sabha in debating on amendments to the Constitution.	1. Barring a few nominated members, the majority of members in the Lok Sabha are elected. 2. Members of the Lok Sabha are directly elected whereas State Assemblies indirectly elect Members of the Rajya Sabha. 3. The Union Executive is answerable to the Lok Sabha. It is the vote of no confidence in the Lok Sabha that forces a Government to resign. 4. Money Bills can be initiated only in the Lok Sabha. 5. The Lok Sabha does not have to accept the Rajya Sabha's recommendations and amendments on Money Bills. 6. When a matter is being debated in a joint session, in the event of a deadlock, the Lok Sabha is at an advantage because it has more members.

The **State Legislature** is referred to as the Legislative Assembly or the Vidhan Sabha in various states. Only five of the states of the Federation of India have Vidhan Parishad – the State Senate House or the Upper House. These are: Maharashtra, Uttar Pradesh, Jammu & Kashmir, Karnataka, and Bihar.

FUNCTIONS AND POWERS OF PARLIAMENT

1. Parliament makes laws, and the function of the Prime Minister and his Council of Ministers is to enforce them. The Union Parliament can make laws on 97 subjects on the Union List and 47 subjects in the Concurrent List. Besides the right to make laws on subjects in the Concurrent List, the Union Government can also make laws on subjects from the State List in **times of Emergency** and also in times of peace, and on matters relating to international issues. Moreover, the Union Parliament can legislate on **any subject that might have been left out of the three Lists.** This is referred to as the **residuary powers of the Union Parliament**. If there is a conflict between a State law and a Union law then the Union law will prevail.
2. Members of Parliament also have the power to check the Executive – the Prime Minister and his Council of Ministers. Their actions must be such so as to enjoy the confidence of other Members of Parliament otherwise they have to quit office if a vote of no confidence is passed against them. They do this through:

   i) interpellation
   ii) adjournment motion
   iii) vote of no confidence
3. The Legislature exercises financial functions such as managing the finances of the state. Every year the government must make a plan as to how to spend its money so that it does not spend too much more than it earns. It is the work of the Finance Minister and his ministry to prepare this budget and present it to Parliament for its approval at the end of every financial year in February. The budget must show the income and expenditure of the previous year and **a plan of how it proposes to collect money in the following year and what its expenses will be.** The Finance Minister presents this Bill in Parliament as the Finance Bill. The Finance Bill is an estimate of the annual expenditure, contains proposals for taxation, and explains how the government plans to collect money to meet its expenses. The Opposition can show its disapproval of the present government through a token cut in the budget. If the **token cut** is passed by a majority of members in the House, it is as good as a vote of no confidence.
4. Parliament has some electoral functions such as electing the President, Vice-President, and the Speaker.
5. Parliament also has a judicial function possessing the sole right to conduct a trial to impeach the President, should the President violate the Constitution.
6. Parliament also has the right to amend the Constitution.
7. Parliament has **other powers,** like the power to change the name of existing states and alter their territorial boundaries.

BILLS CAN BE OF DIFFERENT TYPES

MONEY BILLS	ORDINARY BILLS
Relating to income and expenditure of government: Proposals to impose or remove taxes, regulate government borrowing i) must be **introduced ONLY** in **the Lok Sabha** ii) introduced by the Finance Minister. iii) Suggestions of the Rajya Sabha need not be accepted. iv) Assent of the President never withheld.	**Any Bill not related to Finance can be:** i) moved in either House. ii) passed only if both Houses of Parliament agree upon it.

PRIVATE Member Bills introduced by any **Member of Parliament**

PUBLIC Member Bills introduced by a government **MP – minister in charge**

LIMITATIONS OF STATE GOVERNMENTS

1. Although the Parliament and the State Legislature can make laws on subjects in the Concurrent List, the Union laws shall prevail in case of a conflict between a Union law and a State law.
2. The Union Government can overrule the authority of the states, both in Emergency and in normal times. If the Rajya Sabha passes a resolution by a two-thirds majority that a subject in the State List is of national importance, Parliament is then empowered to make laws on that subject in the State List.
3. When President's Rule is imposed on a state, Parliament makes laws for the state.
4. When the President declares an Emergency, the powers of the state government are curtailed. The President exercises control over the administration of all the states of the Union. The Governors have to take instructions from the President and act in accordance with the directives issued by the President. Parliament acquires unrestricted power to make laws regarding any state and any subject, even if it is in the State List.

6. Certain Bills on subjects like inter-state trading require the prior permission of the President before they are moved in the House.
7. Some Bills require Presidential assent before becoming a law. Bills regarding the acquisition of public property need the assent of the President.

ANSWERS TO PAGE 83—RECOGNISING PARLIAMENTARY LANGUAGE

Term	Answer
1. Casting vote	c
2. Yield to the floor	h
3. Draw up the agenda	j
4. Point of order	e
5. Quorum	l
6. Adjourn the meeting	k
7. Recognise member on the floor of the House	d
8. Permission of the chair	g
9. Cross the floor	a
10. Summon Parliament	i
11. Prorogue the session	f
12. Deadlock	b

COMMON TERMS

Adjourn the House	Discontinue the session.
Adult franchise	Anyone above the age of 18 years is entitled to vote.
Agenda	A plan for discussion at a meeting.
Arbitrary laws	Unjustified laws made at random to suit a person or body of persons.
Bicameral system	A legislature with two chambers.
Egalitarian	Equal rights for all.
Electoral roll	A list of all citizens who are eligible to vote in the Indian elections.
Casting vote	A vote given to a person to break the tie in voting.
Delimitation Commission	A body specifically set up to determine the size and number of constituencies according to the size of the population.
Constituencies	Areas demarcated with equal units of population so that the ratio between the number of representatives to the legislature and the population is the same for all States.
Cross the floor	Term used to declare that an elected Member of the Legislature has changed parties.
Debate	Discussion in Parliament.
Electorate	Voters.
Equitable	Fair but not necessarily equal.
Franchise	The right to vote.
Permission of the Chair	An MP seeks permission from the Speaker to make a statement.
Point of order	Objection raised by an MP.

Quorum	The minimum number of members required to be present. If the quorum is not complete, decisions taken at the meeting are not valid. One tenth of the total number of members of the House must be present. This applies to both Houses of Parliament.
Scheduled Castes	The underprivileged such as Dalits, as defined by the Constitution.
Single member constituencies	Only **one** member from each constituency elected as a representative.
Unicameral	A legislature with one chamber.
Universal adult **franchise**	Any citizen, over the age of 18 years, irrespective of caste, colour, race, religion, education, income, and sex, has the **right to vote.**
Veto	An overriding vote, if there is no consensus.
Vote of no confidence	A resolution by which the legislators demand that the cabinet or one of the ministers resign.
Voting by secret ballot	Voting in secret so no one can know who a particular voter is voting for.
Yield to the floor	During a debate, the Speaker of the House interrupts a member to allow another Member of Parliament to speak.

THE JUDICIARY

CHECKS AND BALANCES—SHARING OF POWER

A Government with a system of checks and balances is an organisation where the three branches of Government—the Legislature, the Executive and the Judiciary share power and exert some control over the actions of the others. **No one body becomes more powerful than the other**.

I make the laws and I am the chief executive.
I punish those who disobey me.
'How dare you oppose me?
Banish him! Send him to Timbuktu
Better still, make him disappear.'

I make the laws.
I am accountable to no one.
'Sentence first, verdict afterwards.
Off with her head!' said the Queen to Alice.

We the people draw up a Constitution.
We govern ourselves through the rule of law.
We make laws through an elected Legislature.
We execute laws through an elected Executive.
We the people enforce and interpret the laws
through an independent Judiciary.

Answer the following questions:

1. Which of the three rulers governs a democracy?

____

2. Which of the three rulers governs a country as a dictator?

____

3. Which of the three rulers governs as an absolute monarch?

____

4. Which type of government safeguards individual liberty?

____

5. In a democracy, power to govern is divided between three branches of government. Name the three branches and their functions.

____

____

____

6. In a democracy, where can a citizen appeal for justice and make sure his rights are not violated?

____

7. In India, which document includes this right?

____

____

LET'S APPEAL TO THE JUDICIARY

What is the Judiciary?

The Judiciary is the third wing of the Government. Its main function is to **protect the rights and freedom of citizens, administer justice and settle disputes** according to the laws of the Constitution and those enacted by the Legislature.

Justice is possible only if the Judiciary is impartial and unbiased in its decisions. Therefore, it is significant that one of the conditions of a democracy is a Judiciary independent of the Executive and the Legislature.

Answer the following questions:

1. What is the task of the Judiciary?

____

____

2. What would happen if there was no Judiciary?

____

____

3. Name three provisions the Indian Constitution has made to keep the Judiciary independent of the other branches of the Government.

____

____

____

4. Can the Prime Minister and Council of Ministers dismiss Justice XYZ if he gives a judgement that the Prime Minister does not approve of? Give reasons for your answer.

____

____

5. A judge's salary is fixed. Any change that needs to be made is made through an amendment in Parliament. How does that help to keep the Judiciary independent of the lawmakers?

____

____

6. By whom should the judges be selected? How does the selection process influence the independence of the Judiciary?

____

____

7. Why is it important that the Executive does not have the final say in the appointment of judges?

____

____

Think about this

The Constitution represents people's hopes and objectives. The Legislature, an elected body, represents the people. Who should have more power—the Executive, the Legislature or the Judiciary? Give reasons for your answer.

____

____

HOW IS JUDICIAL AUTHORITY EXERCISED?

The Judiciary carries out its functions through a system of national courts administering the laws of the republic and the States.

For justice to be even-handed, there must be more than one court of appeal. If a person feels that he has been wrongly indicted in the first trial, he should have the right to appeal to a higher court. The framers of our Constitution decided on a single integrated Judiciary—a tiered system of trial courts. They preferred a single integrated Judiciary to the dual system of justice adopted in the United States.

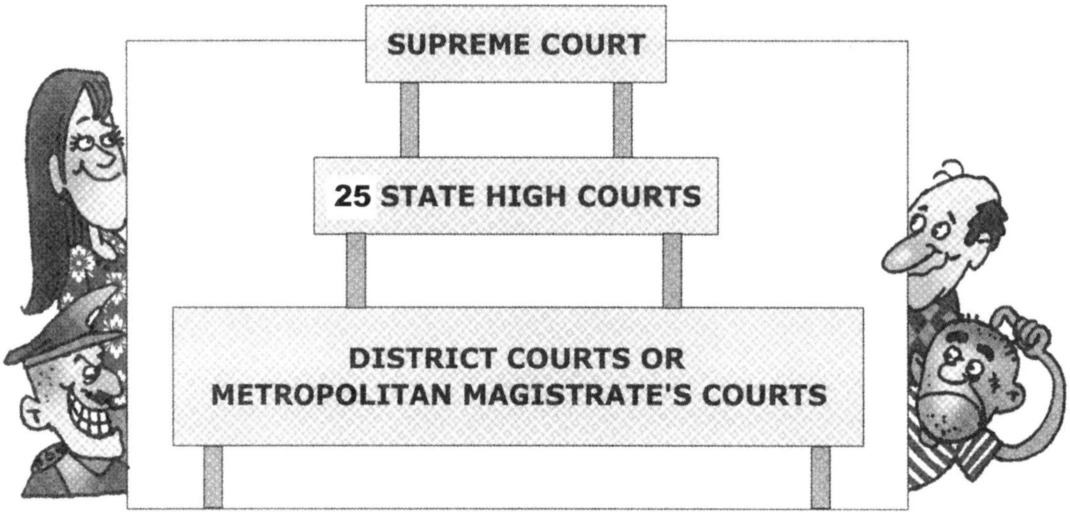

Study the diagram and complete the following sentences.

1. A tiered system of trial courts is ______________________________

____

____

2. The highest court of trials is ______________________________

____

3. The Supreme Court hears cases of appeal from the ______________________________

4. The lowest court for trial is ______________________________

5. The High Court hears cases of appeal from ______________________________

- The Supreme Court is at the head of all courts in India. The head of the Supreme Court is the Chief Justice of India.
- The High Court stands at the head of the State's judicial administration. The head of a State High Court is the Chief Justice of a State.
- Each State is divided into judicial districts presided over by a judge known as the District and Sessions Judge. He is the highest judicial authority in a district. In the administration of civil matters, there are judicial officers under him known as munsifs, sub-judges, civil judges. When he handles criminal cases, the same judge is known as the sessions judge. In the administration of criminal law, there is a chief judicial magistrate and judicial magistrates of first and second class under him.

How does the dual system of courts work in the United States?

Examine the diagram and answer the questions that follow.

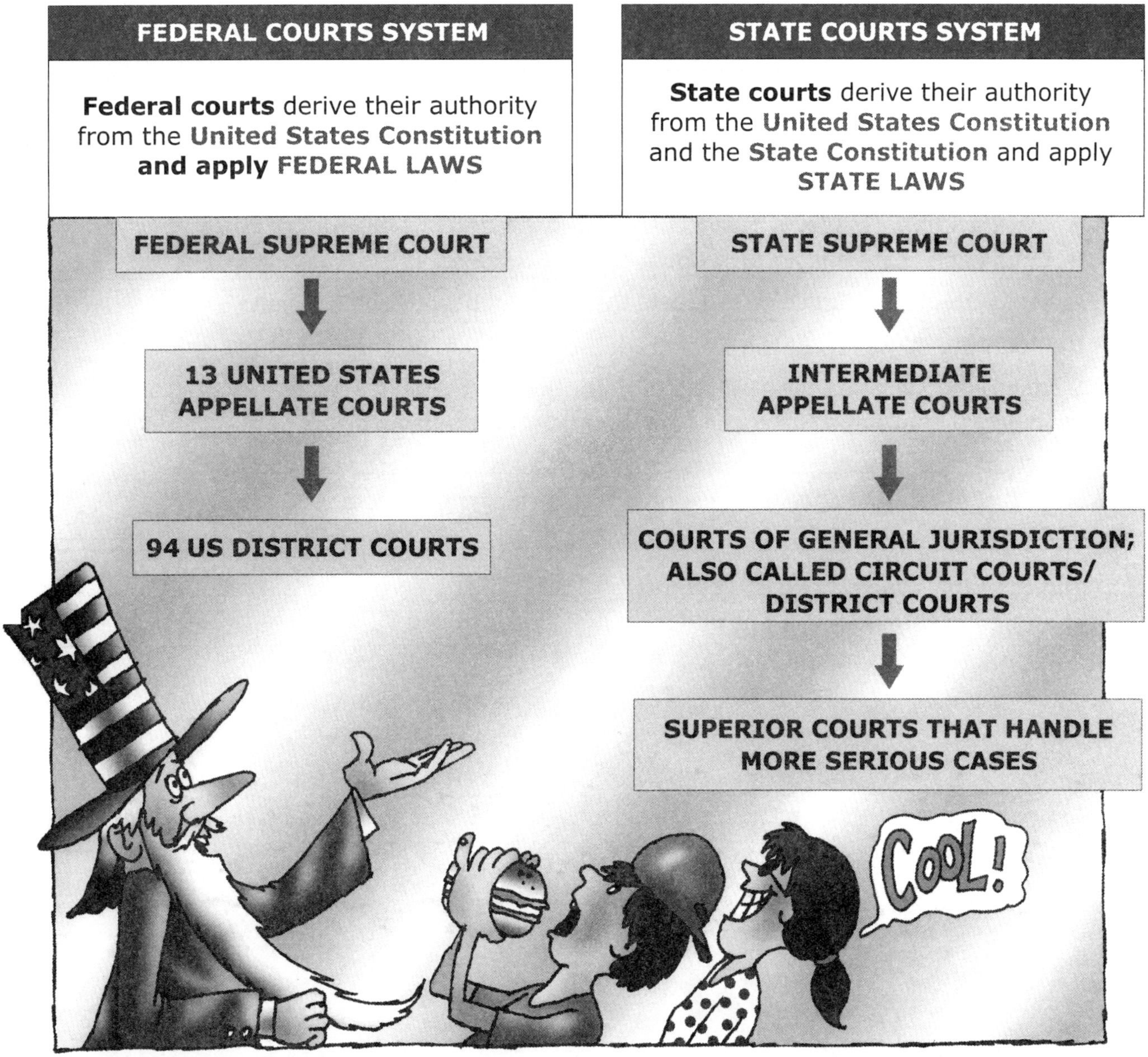

1. How many Constitutions exist in the United State's system of justice?

2. Which laws do the Federal Courts of the United States apply in their hearing?

3. Which laws do the State Circuit Courts apply?

4. Can a case from the State Supreme Court be appealed to in the US Supreme Court?

5. After a case has been lost in the State Circuit Court which is the next court a person can appeal to?

Refer to pages 112-119

Say whether these statements are true or false.

1.	In India each State has its own Constitution.	
2.	A single integrated Judiciary suggests that judicial power is centralised.	
3.	In India, the same law of the Constitution is applied in all the States of the federation.	
4.	In India, the laws of a State can vary according to the laws a State Legislature enacts.	
5.	The State High Court has to apply only the laws of the State and not the Constitution.	
6.	There are 28 High Courts in India.	
7.	The Supreme Court is the apex court.	

COURT JURISDICTIONS—WHO JUDGES WHAT?

What is jurisdiction?

By jurisdiction we mean the **claim or right of a court to try a case**. Courts have different types of jurisdiction. A court can have original and/or appellate jurisdiction.

Original Juristiction

Original jurisdiction is the right of the court to hear a case for the first time. It is the court where the case originates.

Appellate Jurisdiction

Appellate jurisdiction is the right of a court to try a case that has already been tried in a lower court. If an individual loses the case in the first trial, he or she has the **right of appeal** to a higher court. The court where appeals are made is referred to as an **appellate court** and the same court has appellate jurisdiction.

The Supreme Court and the High Court have original and appellate jurisdiction.

What kind of cases come up for trial in courts?

Courts hear criminal or civil cases.

Criminal courts hear criminal cases. Criminal cases pertain to crimes such as murder, theft, cheating, blackmail, fraud, forgery and arson. Evasion of tax is a criminal offence. The sentences awarded in criminal courts are fines and prison sentences—short-term, life, and even death sentences. In some cases, the sentence may be both a fine and a prison term. In criminal cases, the complainant is the State itself. This is because a 'crime' is an offence against society at large and not just an individual.

Civil courts settle **civil cases** involving disputes over property, inheritance, breach of contract, marriage, divorce, child custody, damage to property, accidental injury, claims of money and business disputes. Sentences awarded in civil courts are payment for damages to the concerned party. In civil cases, the State is not necessarily a party and a civil case may be between two private parties.

Answer the following questions:

Will the following charges be heard as civil cases or as criminal cases:

	Civil or Criminal
1. A burglar breaks into your house and is under arrest.	
2. A State Government breaks a contract with a foreign multinational company setting up a power plant.	
3. Mrs Armani has been awarded half of her husband's assets in a divorce case but he refuses to pay.	
4. Mr Bhambhani, an industrialist, has not paid income tax for fifteen years.	
5. Mr and Mrs Shah go to court quarrelling over the right of custody of their children.	
6. Mr Jain's son disputes his father's will and sister's claim to half the share of the property.	
7. An actress sues her ex-husband on charges of disfiguring her face after physical abuse.	

Find Out

1. How many judges are there in the Supreme Court? ____________________

2. How many judges are there in the High Courts? ____________________

3. Who decides on the number of judges in the Supreme Court and High Court?

____

____

____

WHO APPOINTS THE JUDGES OF THE SUPREME COURT?

Judges to the Supreme Court are officially appointed by the President but only after consultation with the Chief Justice of the Supreme Court and existing judges of the Supreme Court. In the appointment of the Chief Justice of India, the President shall consult the judges of the High Courts and the Supreme Court. The President, in consulation with the Chief Justice of the High Court, appoints the judges of the High Court. The President administers the oath of office to judges of the Supreme Court. When taking the oath of office, a judge promises to **perform his duties without fear or favour and uphold the Constitution.**

Answer the following questions:

1. Which authority determines the number of judges to be appointed to the Supreme Court?

2. Which authority determines the number of judges to be appointed to the High Court?

3. Name the authority which administers the oath of office to the judges of the Supreme Court and the High Court.

4. Explain what the promise to **'perform his duties without fear or favour and uphold the Constitution'** means?

5. Who should have the final say, the President or the Chief Justice of India, in the appointment of a judge? Give reasons for your answer.

Did You Know?

Indira Gandhi imposed emergency from 1975 to 1977. She looked upon the Constitution and the Judiciary as obstacles in the way of her securing absolute power. As she had two-third majority in Parliament, she succeeded in passing the Twenty-fourth Amendment Act, which gave Parliament the powers to amend any part of the Constitution.

Judges were transferred to inconvenient places. This amendment was challenged in the Supreme Court and it came to be known as the ***Keshavananda Bharti case***. In this matter, the Supreme Court agreed that the Constitution could be amended but ruled that since the Legislature was itself a creation of the Constitution, it had no right to tamper with its 'basic structure'.

This judgement so angered Mrs Gandhi that the very next day she appointed A.N.Roy, a judge whom she favoured, as Chief Justice of India, ahead of J.M. Shelat, K.S. Hegde and A.N. Grover. Mrs Gandhi thus broke the traditional rule of appointing the seniormost judge of the Supreme Court as the Chief Justice.

In 1979, a petition was filed seeking clarification on the method of choosing judges. The Supreme Court ruled that the Government does not need the consent of the Chief Justice in such appointments, though he must be consulted.

By 1982, in the case of *S. P. Gupta and Others vs Union of India*, a seven-member bench of the Supreme Court ruled that in a conflict, the Executive should have the last say on judicial appointments.

In 1993, Justice Venkatachaliah immediately reversed the Gupta judgement. A nine-member bench realised that the independence of the Judiciary would have to be safeguarded not merely by providing security of tenure and other conditions of service after appointment, but also by preventing political influences in making the appointments. This reduced the role of the Executive, and the final opinion to appoint the Chief Justice rested in the hands of the Judiciary.

Which judgements aimed at keeping the Judiciary independent and maintaining the separation of powers?

THE GUARDIAN OF THE CONSTITUTION—THE JUDICIARY

The oath of office of a judge reads as follows:

I XYZ having been appointed as Chief Justice (or a judge) of the Supreme Court swear in the name of God, that I will bear true faith and allegiance to the Constitution of India as by law established; that I shall uphold the sovereignty and integrity of India; that I will duly and faithfully and to the best of my ability, knowledge and judgement perform the duties of my office without fear of favour, affection or ill will and that **I shall uphold the Constitution** and the laws.

Answer the following questions:

1. What does the word allegiance mean?

____

2. To whom or what does the judge swear allegiance? What is the duty of a judge as given in the oath?

____

3. Who is the judge accountable to? Who established the Constitution?

____

4. How shall he perform these duties?

____

____

Does judicial independence mean that judges always give perfect judgement?

WHO WILL JUDGE A JUDGE?

Read the newspaper headlines given in the box below.

What do these headlines suggest?

- 'PM calls for Introspection on Judicial Appointments'
- 'A Rough Justice'
- 'UP Cops want CBI Probe against 34 Judges'
- 'How to Judge a Judge'
- 'Judging the Judge'

In 1993, in reaction to Indira Gandhi's arbitrary decisions regarding judges, a nine judge bench of the Supreme Court laid down a new system for making appointments of judges to the High Court and Supreme Court. It gave enormous power to a collegium of senior judges of the Supreme Court to select and make recommendations to the Government for the appointment of judges. Their recommendations were also binding on the Government and President. Thus the Judiciary enjoys enormous power without any accountability, particularly the arbitrary power to appoint anyone it chooses.

Which aspect of a democratic government has not been maintained in the appointment of judges?

____

____

What has this led to?

____

____

Write your opinion about the following suggestion by a former Union Law Minister.

A National Judicial Commission to be formed as a permanent body for the appointment and removal of judges. It should consist of the following five members:

- A chairman to be nominated by all judges of the Supreme Court
- A member to be nominated by all the chief justices of High Courts
- A member to be nominated by the Union Cabinet

- A member to be nominated by the leader of the opposition in the Lok Sabha, in consulation with the leaders of different opposition groups in the two houses of Parliament;
- The fifth member could be nominated by a committee of the chairman of the Rajya Sabha, Speaker of the Lok Sabha and Attorney General of India.

Discuss how this could help to maintain a system of checks and balances and make judges accountable?

HOW WILL YOU JUDGE A JUDGE?

Can a judge be removed from office?

A judge cannot be removed from office except by an order of the President. Such a procedure is called **impeachment**. Each House of Parliament must pass a resolution proving the judge's misbehaviour. Misbehaviour could be such acts as accepting bribes, misusing power, acting against the provisions of the Constitution. The Constitution states that the resolution for impeachment must meet two conditions.

The resolution for removal of a judge has to be supported in each house:

- **by a vote of the majority of its total membership AND**
- **by a majority of no less than two-thirds of its members present and voting.**

1. To fulfil the first condition, **a majority of its total membership, that is 51% of the house, must vote for the resolution**. If there are 540 members in Lok Sabha, the resolution for a judge's removal must be passed by at least 271 members.
2. To fulfil the second condition, **two-thirds of the members present and voting** on the day the resolution is passed must vote for the resolution.
   - If there is a full house of 540 members, then two-thirds of the members will be 360, and 360 votes will be required to pass the resolution.
   - If there are only 250 members present on that day, then the votes of two-thirds of the members present, that is, 166 votes, are not enough to pass the resolution. A minimum of 271 votes must be cast.
   - If there are 400 members present at the time of voting, then the votes of more than two-thirds of the members—266 votes—are not enough to pass the resolution. The resolution has to be passed by at least 271 votes and by two-thirds of the total number of members of the house, thus meeting both conditions.

Impeachment is not an easy process. The Lok Sabha failed to prove the case against Justice Ramaswami because the ruling Government abstained from voting and therefore the resolution could not be passed. Subsequently, he resigned from office.

Is impeachment a strong enough check on Judges' behaviour?

Accountability

Judges have to be independent, but they have to be accountable. To whom should they be accountable—the Government or the people?

Will criticism and comment by the media be considered contempt?

To uphold the dignity of the Judiciary, the Constitution has vested the Supreme Court with power to punish for the contempt of court.

Contempt of court is an act of defiance of the court's authority or dignity. Contempt of court can be direct swearing at a judge or violence against a court officer. It can be wilful disobedience of any judgement or order of the High Court and Supreme Court. The punishment for contempt is a fine or a brief stay in jail. Even a judge can commit contempt of his own court, for example, if he swears at a lawyer appearing before him or throws a shoe at him.

In which of the following instances is a judge within his rights in using the contempt clause? Mark with ✓ or ✗

1. Speaking disrespectfully to the judge during a court hearing.	
2. Refusing to obey a court order issued to ex-government officers and ministers to vacate government houses they have been occupying after their term of office.	
3. Writing an article about the Judiciary in general, saying that judges have become susceptible to corruption, and that people have lost faith in the Judiciary.	
4. Publishing an article that specifically slanders a particular judge.	
5. Making a remark in public that the Judiciary has not examined all the evidence in a particular case.	
6. A judge calling a lawyer names in court and telling him to get out.	

Do you as an Indian citizen have the right to disagree with judicial opinion? How will you express your opinion?

HOW WILL YOU DECIDE WHO MAKES A GOOD JUDGE?

Who is qualified to be a judge of the Supreme Court?
According to the Constitution:

- He or she must be a citizen of India
- He or she must have been a judge of a High Court for at least five years or
- He or she must have practised as an advocate in any State High Court for at least ten years
- If in the opinion of the President, a person is a distinguished jurist, a scholar in law, he or she is eligible for the office

What do you think?

What kind of person makes a good judge? Write a paragraph on what you would look for in a person before appointing him or her as a judge?

THE SUPREME COURT— I AM THE FINAL AUTHORITY

The Supreme Court of India is located in New Delhi. It is the final court of appeal. A judgement served by the Supreme Court cannot be reversed. One of its most important powers is **judicial review**.

Answer the following questions:

1. Which is the highest law of the land?

___

2. Who do you think has the final word on the interpretation of that law?

___

What is judicial review?

The Constitution vests the Supreme Court with the authority to review laws made in Parliament and State Legislatures, executive orders and ordinances to check whether they conform to the articles of the Constitution. It also reviews the actions of the Government and the administration. If any law or action is inconsistent with the Constitution, it is declared ultra vires or null and void. The Supreme Court has the **final authority to interpret** the Constitution. When interpreting the Constitution, the Supreme Court considers the intentions of the Constitution makers and the aims of the Constitution. Only the Supreme Court has the right to review its own judgements and to revise its earlier decisions. The court could declare governmental actions unconstitutional. The minimum number of judges required to hear a case involving an interpretation of the Constitution is five.

The arbitrary power of the Executive and the Legislature, a Prime Minister or President and the Parliament can be checked through a Supreme Court decision made after a judicial review.

The judgements in the Golaknath and Keshavananda Bharati cases are examples of the Supreme Court using its powers of **judicial review**. Judges can only review laws or other governmental acts that are challenged in court.

TUG OF WAR: MRS GANDHI VS THE SUPREME COURT, 1971

Can Parliament amend Article 13 of the Constitution?

Article 13: The State shall not make any law, which takes away or abridges the Fundamental Rights conferred by the Constitution, and any law made in contravention of this clause shall, to the extent of the contravention, be void.

'Abolish the privy purses[1] promised to rulers of Princely States in return for surrendering their sovereignty at the time of Independence. Nationalise banks! The aims of the Directive Principles of State Policy to bring about social and economic justice are more important than the Right to Property.'

How did the Supreme Court use its power of judicial review to interpret and uphold the Constitution?

'We declare this abolition null and void. The Right to Property is a Fundamental Right.'

Through the verdict on the ***Golaknath case***, the Supreme Court struck down the President's order derecognising the princes. 'In giving the Constitution to themselves, the people had reserved the Fundamental Rights for themselves.' **Article 13** expressed this limitation on the powers of Parliament to modify, restrict or impair fundamental freedoms.

[1]The privy purses were sums of money that the Government promised the princely rulers (maharajas) in return for joining the Union of India at the time of Independence in 1947.

After this judgement, Indira Gandhi dissolved Parliament, called for elections again and won two-thirds of the parliamentary seats. A Bill seeking to restore the supremacy of Parliament's power to amend the Constitution was introduced, debated and passed because she had the support of the majority of the members. Parliament restored for itself the absolute power to amend any part of the Constitution including Part III, dealing with Fundamental Rights.

'Since our Constitution and the Judiciary are not in accordance with changing circumstances, Government has decided to terminate the privy purses and privileges of the rulers of the former Indian states through the 26th Amendment Act amending Article 368 and Article 13 of the Constitution.'

Answer the following questions:

1. Who won this round of battle on the supremacy of Parliament vis-à-vis power of the courts to interpret and uphold the Constitution?
2. How did Indira Gandhi bypass the verdict of the Judiciary?
3. What justification did she give for amending the Constitution?

Between July 1971 and June 1972, during Mrs Gandhi's tenure as Prime Minister, Parliament made seven amendments to the Constitution. The validity of these amendments to the Constitution was challenged before a full bench of the Supreme Court (thirteen judges). All judges upheld the validity of the Twenty-fourth Amendment saying that Parliament had the power to amend any or all provisions of the Constitution. However, they were clear that Parliament could not use its amending powers under Article 368 to damage, weaken, destroy, abrogate, change the **basic structure** or framework of the Constitution.

The basic structure of the Constitution cannot be changed—Keshavanada Bharati judgement.

The Indian Constitution is flexible and can be amended, but is should not be amended in a manner where the Executive branch of the Government corners power as it happened in 1974.

What constitutes 'basic features'?

There was no unanimity among the judges on what constituted 'basic features'. These were the features the judges thought were basic to the framework of the Constitution and should not be amended:

• republican and democratic form of Government	• Secular character of the Constitution
• separation of powers between the Legislature, the Executive and the Judiciary	• federal character of the Constitution
• the Directive Principles of State Policy with objectives to build a welfare state	• unity and integrity of the nation
• sovereignty of India	• Fundamental Rights
• the individual freedoms secured to the citizens	• Parliamentary form of Government

List according to your priority the features of the Constitution that you think make up the basic structure of the Constitution and should not be changed. You could include other features from the Constitution that are not mentioned above.

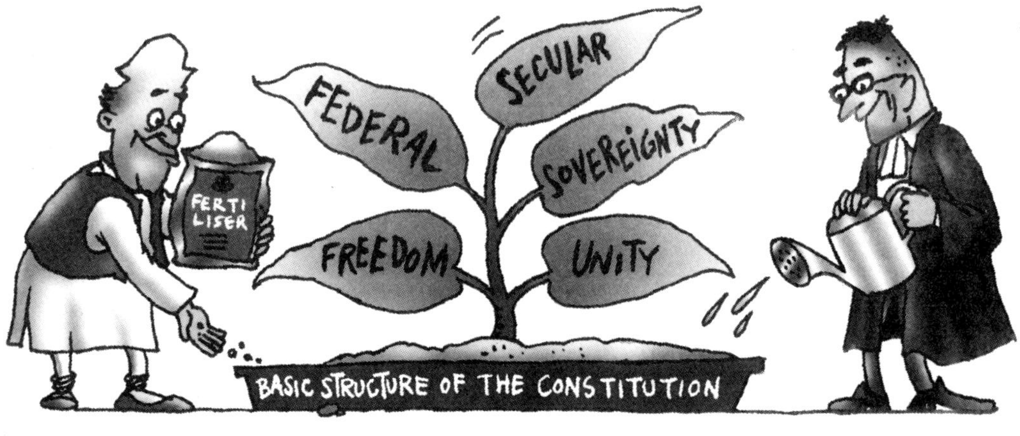

JURISDICTION OF THE SUPREME COURT AND HIGH COURTS

The Supreme Court and High Courts can hear **civil** and **criminal** cases. It has **original, appellate, writ, advisory and revisory jurisdiction** and the power of **judicial review**.

Original jurisdiction exclusive to the Supreme Court

> **Article 131** of the Constitution confers exclusively on the Supreme Court the right of jurisdiction over any dispute:
> 1. between the Government of India and one or more States;
> 2. between the Government of India and any State on one side against one or more States on the other; and
> 3. between two or more States.

Which of the three cases can be heard **only** by the Supreme Court directly?

Mark with a

1. A dispute between a State Government and a company located in the same State over non-payment of local taxes.	
2. A petition filed by lawyers against a State Government for being denied access to information in a State where there is no law and order due to communal riots.	
3. A dispute between States A and B over the sharing of waters of a river flowing through both States.	

Courts have different types of jurisdiction. Given in the table below are names of different courts and different types of jurisdiction the courts handle. Write the appropriate name in Column 2 of the table on the next page.

1.	High Court	8.	Supreme Court
2.	Sessions Court	9.	Civil Court
3.	Metropolitan Courts	10.	Family Courts
4.	Original jurisdiction	11.	Appellate jurisdiction
5.	Advisory jurisdiction	12.	Writ jurisdiction
6.	Jurisdiction to act as a court of record	13.	Revisory jurisdiction
7.	Public interest litigation	14.	Judicial review

Column 1	Column 2
1. A court that hears a case to settle a property dispute.	
2. A petition filed by a third party on behalf of others seeking the realisation of Fundamentals Rights such as women's organisations seeking equal rights for women labourers denied equal pay as men labourers.	
3. An instance of the Supreme Court calling for a case to be transferred to itself.	
4. A district court that tries to determine if a crime has been committed.	
5. In metropolitan cities these courts try criminal cases.	
6. Keshavananda Bharati case used as a precedent for future reference.	
7. The authority of a court to be the first to hear a case.	
8. The authority of a court to give an opinion when the President asks for a clarification.	
9. The authority of a court to hear a case coming up from the lower courts.	
10. The authority of a court to issue orders to enforce Fundamental Rights.	
11. The power of a court to ensure that the new laws are not against the ideals and objectives of the Constitution.	
12. This court has original jurisdiction in all cases between the State and the Union Government.	
13. This court hears cases of appeal from the district court.	
14. This court hears family matters such as divorce cases.	

WHAT IS WRIT JURISDICTION?

A writ is a written order issued by a court to a judicial officer to carry out different types of orders. Through a writ a court may demand that property be returned, that a sentence passed be delivered or enforced, or even that rights hitherto denied to an individual or an organisation be restored. The Supreme Court has wide powers to **issue these writs for the protection of Fundamental Rights in Part III**. The right to approach the Supreme court for a writ is itself a Fundamental Right. The High Courts also have the same powers to issue these writs. They may do so not only for the enforcement of the Fundamental Rights, but for any other purpose too.

Part III of the Constitution—Article 32—guarantees Fundamental Rights to citizens and persons within India. The Right to Constitutional Remedies empowers the Supreme Court or High Courts to issue directions or orders or writs to enforce these rights. The Judiciary during Mrs Gandhi's tenure had ruled that during an emergency this right was not enforceable. The following is an example of a writ.

Wednesday, 11 August 1999
HC NOTICES ON AHMEDABAD RIOTS
PRESS TRUST OF INDIA

AHMEDABAD, AUG 10: The Gujarat High Court has issued notices to the State Government and police commissioner on a **public interest litigation** (PIL) alleging police atrocities on Milatnagar residents during the recent riots in Ahmedabad.

A division bench comprising Chief Justice K.G. Balakrishnan and Justice M.S. Parikh on Monday adjourned the matter for further hearing to 18 August.

The petitioner alleged that on 29 July, the residents of Milatnagar, on the outskirts of the city, were attacked by a mob. The petitioner, besides demanding compensation for damage to property and injuries to residents, has sought institution of a high-level enquiry into the alleged partisan role of the police during the violence at Milatnagar.

1. Which court issued the order?

____

2. To whom was the order issued?

____

3. What did the petitioners ask for?

____

Supreme Court Bans Smoking in Public Places

The Supreme Court of India has directed all States and Union Territories to immediately issue orders banning smoking in public places. The court defined a public place as bus stops, trains, public transport, hospitals, health institutes, public offices, court buildings, educational institutions, libraries and auditoriums.

The interim order by the court came on a public interest litigation seeking a ban on smoking filed by Congress leader Murli Deora. The petition sought a directive to ban sale of cigarettes and tobacco products to persons below the age of 18. The court adjourned the matter for six weeks.

Of the estimated 3 million tobacco-related deaths a year in the world, nearly one-third take place in India.

1. Who filed the petition? ______________________________

2. What did the petitioner ask for? ______________________________

3. What is an interim order? ______________________________

4. Which Fundamental Right do you think was involved that the Supreme Court admitted this petition for hearing? (Refer to Article 21)

____

5. What is public interest litigation?

____

____

____

____

WHY PUBLIC INTEREST LITIGATION?

The Promise

The Constitution of India guarantees **equal rights to all citizens, irrespective of race, gender, religion** and other considerations, and the Directive Principles of State Policy stress that the Government provide to all citizens a minimum standard of living. The Constitution promises to secure for all its citizens, social, economic and political justice.

The Reality

Read the newspaper. Give three examples of how the promise has not been fulfilled in the years post Independence, especially in the field of providing food, shelter, health, education, and preventing exploitation of women and children.

The Remedy

Ordinarily, the proceedings in the Supreme Court arise out of the judgements or orders made by the subordinate courts including the High Courts. Realising that the poor are at a disadvantage, not having the capacity to represent themselves, or to engage lawyers, the Supreme Court has since 1982 started hearing matters which are in the interest of the public. The Fundamental Rights in Articles 14 and 21 (the Right to Equality and the Right to Life) were interpreted to include the Right to Live with Dignity which in turn means the Right to Health Care, Right to Education, Right to Adequate Means of Livelihood. The Right to Life includes a healthy environment. The court can be moved by any individual or group of persons on behalf of an aggrieved person or persons either by filing a Writ Petition at the filing counter of the court or by addressing a letter to the Honourable Chief Justice of India. The petition seeks the court's intervention in a matter where another party's Fundamental Rights are being violated. Such litigation is known as **public interest litigation** or PIL.

In recent years, the courts have ruled on many issues that might have been given up as lost causes.

1. They have ordered two municipal corporations to clean up garbage in their cities.

2. They have closed down pollution-spreading factories around the famous Taj Mahal.

3. In 1994, when Indian soldiers in Kashmir laid siege to a historic mosque and cut off food supplies to militants holed up inside, Chief Justice Mushaber Ahmadi ordered the army and police to provide the militants with meals.

4. *Vishaka* & *Ors* (petitioners) Vs *State of Rajasthan* & *Ors* (respondents) was a public interest case that came up before the Supreme Court of India at the instance of certain social activists and non-governmental organisations seeking to prevent sexual harassment of working women in all workplaces. Their grievance was that while working women remained prone to harassment in the workplace, neither the Legislature nor the Executive was taking any effective preventive measure on this matter.

5. The Bombay High Court directed that no more trees could be felled for the purposes of putting up hoardings in the city. In a continuation of its earlier order, the court also directed that no hoardings could be erected anywhere in the city till further orders. The order was passed by a division bench comprising Chief Justice C.K. Thakker and Justice S. Radhakrishnan in response to a public interest litigation filed by Dr Anahita Pandole, seeking directions against hoardings in the city. Dr Pandole's petition was supported by several citizen's groups. They include Action for Good Governance and Networking in India, Citipace, D.N.Road Heritage Mile Association and Clean Air and Friends of Trees who filed intervention applications.

For each of these litigations, which Fundamental Right had the person or people been deprived of?

Send a petition

In your neighbourhood, the municipality has failed to clear the garbage on the streets for two months. File a petition seeking a court order against the municipality.

1. Will you file this petition in the Supreme Court or in a High Court?

___

2. What relief will you ask for?

___

3. Which writ might the court issue to demand that the municipality performs its duties?

___

4. Which Fundamental Right are you invoking?

___

Public interest litigation is one way of bringing the courts nearer to the people. There is a common saying, 'Justice delayed is justice denied'. The common man is denied access to legal assistance because of the high cost and delays in legal procedure. Other ways of making the judicial system more accessible to people is through Lok Adalats and Family Courts.

1. Why have Lok Adalats been established?

___

2. What kind of cases do they handle?

___

3. How are they different from regular courts?

___

4. What sort of cases do Family Courts handle?

___

Find Out

Which Act has realised the aim of free legal advice as promised in the Directive Principles of State Policy?

WHOSE JOB IS IT ANYWAY?

The basic role of the Judiciary is to settle disputes between individuals, between individuals and the Government, between individuals and institutions according to the provisions of the Constitution and rule of law as laid down by Parliament. It also interprets the Constitution.

WHAT DO THESE HEADLINES SUGGEST ABOUT THE SUPREME COURT'S ROLE?

When the going gets tough, the Executive Courts the Judiciary

A Legal Fix for Every Ill

Judiciary is Interfering Where There is No Issue Relating to Law

- No bursting of crackers on Deepavali.
- Ban smoking in public places.
- Order the use of compressed natural gas (CNG) by taxis and buses instead of petrol or diesel and penalise them if not done within the time limit.

No doubt there is a Fundamental Right to clean air involved in these orders, but in terms of actually implementing the order, is it practial? Why can't these orders pronounced by the Judiciary be enforced easily? What are the complications in carrying out these orders?

Who should be passing laws for the protection of women against harassment in the workplace?

Who should be ensuring that the law banning the cutting down of trees is executed?

Who should have made the decision on whether the bhoomi pooja in Ayodhya should have been held given the political unrest at the time?

Whose job is it to maintain law and order?

The Judiciary is doing the work of the Legislature and the Executive. The Executive does not want to take decisions on sensitive issues like Ayodhya that might lose them votes in the next election. If the Executive and the Legislature do not discharge their duties, someone has to take responsibility.

What is the danger to democracy if the courts become too activist?

LET'S SUM IT UP

How are power and responsibility distributed, shared and limited in the Government established by the Indian Constitution?

In the box below, points A-F list the constitutional provisions pertaining to the power of the Government. Below the box are two columns. Column A lists certain situations. In Column B, list the constitutional provisions that match with situations given in Column A. The first one has been done for you.

A. The Right to Constitutional Remedies: Fundamental Rights can be enforced through a court of law. People check the abuse of power by Government.

B. A federal structure of Government: Power is divided between State and Union Government, and one acts as a check on the other.

C. A parliamentary democracy: There are two heads of State: de facto and de jure.

D. A bicameral Legislature: The Upper and Lower House keep a check on each other.

E. An independent Judiciary: It keeps a check on the laws enacted by the Legislature, and prevents the misuse of power by the Executive.

F. Impeachment: Parliament can check the abuse of judicial and executive power by judges or the President using its power of impeachment.

Column A: Situations	Column B
1. Individuals can file a petition in the Supreme Court if their Right to Life had been threatened when a State Government has been ineffective in quelling riots.	**1-A** The Right to Constitutional Remedies
2. The Union Government, through the use of Article 356, can impose President's Rule on a State where law and order has broken down.	
3. A TV channel can file a petition in the Supreme Court to enforce its Right to Freedom of the Press when it is prevented by a State Government from reporting news on a communal riot.	

Column A: Situations	Column B
4. All bills have to be passed in both houses. The Upper House acts as a check on laws being hastily passed.	
5. Members to the Rajya Sabha are elected by the State Legislative Assemblies. The Rajya Sabha is the voice of all the States of the Union.	
6. A procedure for impeachment of Judge ABC is initiated in the Lok Sabha to control the misuse of his office for personal gain.	
7. A judge's salary is fixed and cannot be changed at the whims of the Legislature. Any change in the judge's salary has to be through an amendment of the Constitution.	
8. The President cannot call for President's Rule in a State unless the Council of Ministers with the Prime Minister at the head, aids and advises the President.	
9. In 1997, President Narayanan asked the United Front Government to reconsider their decision to use Article 356 to dismiss the Kalyan Singh Government in Uttar Pradesh. He said that according to the rule of law, first, a confidence vote on the floor of the State's Legislative Assembly was necessary.	

Do you know of any real-life situations where constitutional checks have not worked?

FACTS

Provisions made by the Indian Constitution to ensure that the Judiciary is independent of the Executive and the Legislature

Security of service: The Indian Constitution guarantees security of service to all judges. A judge retires at 65 in the Supreme Court and at the age of 62 in the High Courts. Judges of the Supreme Court and High Court cannot be dismissed at the whim of a new Government, or a Prime Minister or Chief Minister or any minister. A judge cannot be removed from office except by an order of the President after each House of Parliament has passed a resolution proving the judge's misbehaviour. Misbehaviour could be such acts as accepting bribes, misusing power, acting against the provisions of the Constitution. Such a procedure is referred to as **impeachment.** An impeachment is a trial in Parliament to remove a person in very high office like the president or a judge. There is a special process for impeachment.

Security of income: This is assured through fixed salaries. A **judge's salary is fixed** and is charged to the Consolidated Fund of India. Any change in the judge's salary has to be through an amendment of the Constitution. The Legislature cannot intimidate the Judiciary into changing its judgement by voting for a cut in a judge's salary.

The Consolidated Fund is made up of all revenue collected as taxes, duties, raised as loans. The money from this fund is used for Government expenditure as specified in the Constitution.

An adequate income and an adequate pension: Judges must be paid an adequate income and pension suitable to the dignity of their office. This will discourage judges from being influenced into giving biased judgements in favour of persons or organisations that promise remuneration in cash or kind, or employment after retirement. In some countries, judges are never retired for this reason. Earlier, judges earned salaries in the range of Rs 10,000-12,000 and salaries were frozen for thirty-seven years at amounts fixed on 26 January 1950. The effect of this freeze was felt on the calibre of judges in the High Courts and the Supreme Court. This was recognised by the Fifty-fourth Amendment Act, 1986, which substantially raised the salaries of judges.

THE JUDICIAL SYSTEM IN INDIA

In India, there is only one Constitution that applies to the different states of the Union. Unlike the dual system of justice in the United States, we have a **single integrated Judiciary, a tiered system**. The Supreme Court is the highest court of trial. Subordinate to it are the State High Courts and subordinate to them are the District Courts in each State. Thus the case is first heard in the District Court or in the Metropolitan Magistrate's Court if in a city. If the person loses the case in the lower court, he or she can appeal to the High Court. If the case is lost in the High Court, an appeal can be made to the Supreme Court of India, but the Supreme Court does not necessarily admit all cases.

It was decided that India would adopt a single integrated Judiciary to have more uniformity in law to maintain the unity of the country, and to support a more centralised form of Government. Even though India is a federation, the Union Government has more power than the States which make up the federation.

The following table compares the Supreme Court and High Courts with reference to:

1. Authority that establishes the courts
2. Number of courts
3. Appointment of judges
4. Tenure of office
5. Number of judges
6. Administration of oath of office
7. Qualifications for becoming a judge

CRITERIA	SUPREME COURT	HIGH COURT
1. Authority that establishes the courts	The Constitution.	The Constitution. **Parliament by law can** establish one High Court for two or more States.
2. Number of courts	One.	Twenty five The State High Courts are **subordinate to the Supreme Court of India.** Three courts have jurisdiction over more than one State: i) Mumbai High Court has jurisdiction over Maharashtra, Goa, Dadra and Nagar Haveli, and Daman and Diu. ii) Guwahati High Court has jurisdiction over Assam, Manipur, Meghalaya, Nagaland, Tripura, Mizoram and Arunachal Pradesh. iii) Punjab and Haryana High Court has jurisdiction over Punjab, Haryana and Chandigarh.

3. Appointment of judges	President in consultation with the Chief Justice of the Supreme Court and existing judges of the Supreme Court.	President in consultation with the Chief Justice of the High Court.
4. Tenure of office	Retirement at age 65.	Retirement at age 62. After retirement, a judge can plead only in the Supreme Court or any High Court other than the one where he held office.
5. Number of judges	The Constitution originally stipulated that the Supreme Court should comprise seven judges and a Chief Justice. Through subsequent amendments, the maximum number of judges that can be appointed is now 31. The Constitution also provides for appointments of more judges on an ad hoc basis for specific cases such as an inquiry into police firing during a riot.	No limit. Decided by the President according to the volume of work.
6. Administration of oath of office	President.	Governor of the State.
7. Qualifications for becoming a judge	The person: (a) is a citizen of India, (b) has been a judge of a High Court for at least five years, or (c) has practised as a lawyer in any State High Court for at least ten years, (d) is a distinguished jurist, learned in law.	The person: (a) is a citizen of India, (b) has practised as a lawyer in a State High Court for at least ten years, (c) has held a judicial office for not less than ten years.

Subordinate Courts

Each state is divided into several districts which have their own courts subordinate to State High Courts. The courts that try civil cases are referred to as **District Courts** and the courts that hear criminal cases are called **Sessions Courts**. A district judge hears civil cases and criminal cases. When he hears civil cases he is referred to as the district judge. When he hears criminal cases he is referred to as the Sessions judge. Subordinate to the District Court are courts of the subordinate judge, senior sub-judge and munsif. These courts deal with civil disputes not involving more than Rs 5,000. A munsif's court deals with civil cases involving not more than Rs 2,000. The sentences awarded in criminal courts are prison sentences, short-term and life imprisonment, and death sentences.

The Governor in consultation with the High Court makes the appointment of district judges, both civil and sessions. Appointments of district judges without consulting the High Court are illegal. To be **eligible** for appointment as a district judge, **civil or sessions**, a person must have been:

1. A pleader or an advocate for at least seven years.
2. A judicial officer of the Union or State Governments.

Besides judicial magistrates in the Sessions Courts, there are **executive magistrates** who are responsible for maintaining law and order and preventing crime, and are responsible for the administrative work in the district. **They do not try cases**. The State Government makes their appointment and they are **subordinate to the State Government officials and not the High Court.** The reason for appointing executive magistrates is to ensure that **executive and judicial power are separated** so that the executive power of the State Government does not influence judicial officers in the dispensation of justice.

A city which has a population of more than 10 lakh is referred to as a metropolitan city. In such cities, besides the District Civil and Sessions Courts and subordinate to High Courts are the **Small Causes Courts** and **Metropolitan Magistrates Courts. Small Causes Courts** try cases which involve amounts of Rs 25,000 and less. The **Metropolitan Magistrates Courts** handle criminal cases.

Considering the backlog of cases, it has been considered necessary to create informal courts to distribute the workload to District Courts to ensure quick justice. The High Court can transfer its cases to courts other than district or city civil courts.

Lok Adalats: Lok Adalat means people's court, in contrast to the regular law courts established by the Government. These courts have been established to meet the problems the judicial system in India faces:

1. Inadequate number of courts and judges.
2. Increase in number of cases in recent years due to different Acts enacted by the Central and State Governments.
3. The high cost involved in prosecuting or defending a case in a court of law—heavy court fees, lawyer's fee and incidental charges.
4. Delay in disposal of cases resulting in huge backlog of cases in all courts.

The benefits that litigants derive through the Lok Adalat are many:

1. There is no court fee. If the case is already filed in the regular court, the fee paid will be refunded if the dispute is settled at the Lok Adalat.
2. There is no strict application of the legal procedure. The parties to the dispute, though represented by their advocates, can interact with the Lok Adalat judge directly and explain their stands in the dispute.
3. Disputes can be brought before the Lok Adalat directly instead of going to a regular court first.
4. The decision of the Lok Adalat is binding on the parties to the dispute and its order is capable of execution through legal process. No appeal lies against the order of the Lok Adalat, whereas in the regular law courts there is always a scope to appeal to the higher court on the decision of the trial court, which causes delay in the settlement of the dispute. Since the dispute is resolved by mutual settlement, no case for appeal will arise.

Family Courts settle family disputes and also counsel the parties concerned. The Family Courts Act, 1984 aims at promoting conciliation and securing speedy settlement of disputes relating to marriage and family affairs and related matters.

The Criminal Procedures Act provides for free legal aid at State expense in all criminal cases to persons too poor to afford a lawyer. This provision meets one of the aims of the Directive Principles of State Policy, *right to equal opportunity* and *free legal aid.*

Types of Jurisdiction of the Supreme Court and High Courts

Original Jurisdiction of the Supreme Court: Besides cases involving a State and the Union Government, and cases between two State Governments, the Supreme Court has original jurisdiction over cases:

1. Relating to the constitutional validity of central laws.
2. Expecially related to constitutional matters which it deems necessary to transfer from a subordinate court to itself.
3. Relating to violation of Fundamental Rights. When a citizen invokes his right to constitutional remedies, the Supreme Court enforces these rights by issuing **WRITS, habeas corpus, mandamus, prohibition, quo warranto and certiorari.**

Original Jurisdiction of the High Courts:

1. A High Court of a state has original jurisdiction over cases that concern State laws, revenues, and collection of taxes.
2. It is also the custodian of the Constitution. Like the Supreme Court, the High Court has the right to issue writs to enforce the Fundamental Rights of citizens. The High Courts in states have original jurisdiction over cases involving contempt of court.
3. The High Courts of cities like **Mumbai, Chennai and Kolkata have special power of original jurisdiction over almost every civil or criminal matter**. In other States, criminal matters are first heard by the Sessions judge at the district level, but in these cities, the High Court can try a case without it being tried in a lower court.

Appellate Jurisdiction

An appeal can be made to the **Supreme Court** from any judgement, decree of final order of High Court in the territory of India, whether in a civil, criminal or other proceeding, if the High Court certifies that the case involves an interpretation of the Constitution. Even if the High Court refuses to give such a certificate, the Supreme Court can grant special leave to appeal if it is satisfied that the case involves a substantial question of law as to the interpretation of the Constitution. It admits **appellate criminal** cases when:

1. A High Court withdraws a criminal case from a lower court and convicts a person and gives a sentence of capital punishment.
2. A person has been acquitted by the Sessions Court but convicted in the High Court.
3. A High Court certifies that the case is suitable for appeal to the Supreme Court.

The **appellate jurisdiction of the High Court of States** extends over appeals against the decision of the district judges and other subordinate courts in civil cases. In criminal cases, the High Court will hear only those appeals from the Sessions Court where the sentence of imprisonment awarded by a lower court is for more than seven years.

Advisory Jurisdiction

The President has the authority to seek the advice of the Supreme Court on any question of law. But the Supreme Court cannot be compelled to give the advice and it is not obligatory for the President to follow the advice of the Supreme Court.

Courts of Record

Judgements and directives of the Supreme Court and High Courts are preserved as a record and are used as precedents for future cases. This record has taken the form of 'precedents'. Its judgements are binding on all the courts of India and is applicable to all similar cases. Such judgements are used as a point of reference to decide similar cases in the future. The High Court is also a Court of Record and judgements given in the High Court are used as precedents for future cases.

Revisory Jurisdiction

The Supreme Court can direct transfer of any civil or criminal case from one State High Court to another State High Court or from a court subordinate to another State High Court. If the Supreme Court is satisfied that a case is of general importance, it may withdraw a case or cases pending before the High Court or High Courts and dispose of all such cases itself. If a High Court feels that a case being heard in a subordinate court is linked to constitutional law, the High Court has the right to transfer the case to itself or it can determine the question of law and send the case back to the subordinate court to proceed with the case. The lower court must act in accordance with the opinion of the High Court.

Writ Jurisdiction

The Supreme Court and the High Courts have the power to issue directions or orders or writs, including writs in the nature of habeas corpus, mandamus, certiorari, prohibition and quo warranto, for the enforcement of Fundamental Rights.

DEFINITION OF TERMS

Acquit	Declare a person not guilty.
Acquittal	Verdict that a person is not guilty of the crime he or she has been charged with.
Ad hoc	Latin, 'for specific purpose'. An ad hoc committee is created for specific purpose or task, and once it has studied and reported on the matter, it is disbanded.
Advocate	A professional pleader in a court.
Alimony	An amount given by one spouse to another while they are separated or divorced.
Bail	A temporary release of an accused, usually on deposit of a sum of money to guarantee their appearance at the court at a later date.
Bench	The office of judge or magistrate; judges or magistrates collectively.
Capital punishment	Death penalty for serious criminal offences.
Defamation	An attack on the good reputation of a person by slander or libel.
Defendant	An entity sued or accused in a court of law, also known as the respondent.
Indict	To accuse a person with a serious crime. It is on the basis of an indictment that an accused person must stand trial.
Jury	A group of citizens randomly selected from the general population to assist justice by deciding through the evidence what constitutes 'the truth'.
Litigant	A person fighting a legal case.
Null and void	Not legally binding.
Plaintiff	The person who brings a case to court against another. Other terms: 'claimant', 'petitioner' or 'applicant'.
Solicitor	Member of the legal profession who advises clients and instructs barristers or lawyers but does not generally appear in court.
Subpoena	A writ commanding a person's attendance in court.
Summons	A call to appear before a judge or magistrate.
Trespass	To intrude on another person's land or right.
Verdict	The decision of a jury of guilty or not guilty.
Warrant	An official written document giving authority for an action, such as a warrant for an arrest.
Writs	Written orders from the court. The various writs are as follows: *habeas corpus*: If a person is arrested without being given a reason, the Supreme Court can issue a writ of habeas corpus, requiring the person in custody to be brought before it. It is usually issued in criminal cases in order to determine whether a prisoner is being lawfully held by the police, and if so, what the charges are. It prevents arbitrary imprisonment.

- *Certiorari*: An order from the superior court to an inferior court calling for the proceedings of a case from a lower court to review it.
- *Mandamus*: Latin, 'we command'. A writ issued by a court of superior jurisdiction commanding a lower court, a public official, a corporation, or a private person to perform their duties. The writ is used only to compel a person to carry out an official duty. The person to whom the writ is directed has no choice in the matter.
- *Prohibition*: An order from a superior court to a subordinate court to stop the proceedings in the lower court because the former feels the subordinate court is not being fair, or is prejudiced in the trial.
- *Quo warranto*: A writ challenging a person to show by what authority he claims an office. This is used when an individual makes decisions claiming he has done so in his/her official capacity.

Answers to the quiz on pages 119-120

(1) Civil Court
(2) Public interest litigation
(3) Revisory jurisdiction
(4) Sessions Court
(5) Metropolitan Courts
(6) Jurisdiction to act as a court of record
(7) Original jurisdiction
(8) Advisory jurisdiction
(9) Appellate jurisdiction
(10) Writ jurisdiction
(11) Judicial review
(12) Supreme Court
(13) High Court
(14) Family Courts

Answers to the quiz on pages 127-128

1A: The Right to Constitutional Remedies, whereby Fundamental Rights can be enforced through a court of law. People check the abuse of power by Government.

2B: A federal structure of Government. The Centre checks on the State Goverment.

3A: The Right to Constitutional Remedies.

4D: A bicameral Legislature. The two Houses keep a check on each other.

5B: A federal structure of Government. The States have a voice in the Union Government.

6F: Impeachment. A judge cannot use his official position for personal gain.

7E: An independend Judiciary. The Legislature and the Executive cannot influence judicial decisions by threatening a cut in salary. This allows the Judiciary to keep a check on the laws enacted by the Legislature and acts as a check on the misuse of power by the Executive.

8C: A parliamentary democracy. Two heads of State, de facto and de jure, to keep a check on each other. The Forty-second Amendment to the Constitution says that the President exercises his executive powers on the advice of the Council of Ministers with the Prime Minister at its head.

9C: A parliamentary democracy. Two heads of State. The Forty-fourth Amendment in 1978 gives the President the right to ask the Cabinet to reconsider a desicion. A presidential check on the Cabinet.

OTHER BOOKS YOU MAY LIKE

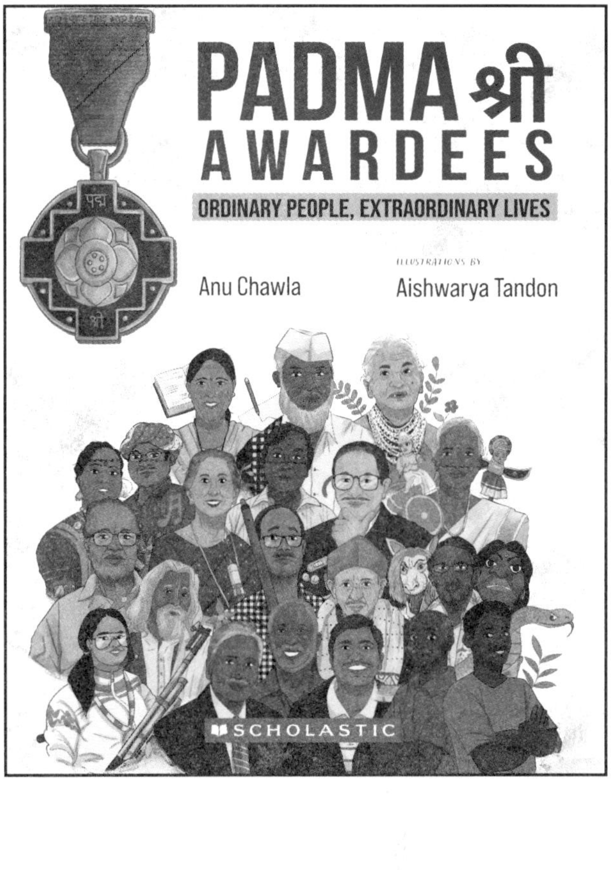